a sky the color of chaos

by M.J. Fievre

**Based on the True Story
of my Haitian Childhood**

Published 2014 by Beating Windward Press LLC

For contact information, please visit:
www.BeatingWindward.com

Text Copyright © M.J. Fievre, 2015
All Rights Reserved
Front Cover Design: Charlotte Howard, CKH Design
Interior & Back Cover Design: Copyright © KP Creative, 2015

Girl's Face on cover: Photograph Courtesy M.J. Fievre
Hand holding ice cream on cover: © 2010 CCPL/Antifluor, "Cape Verde, Santiago Island"
Blue Jumper on cover: Public Domain
Background on cover: © Les Stone Photography, "Port-au-Prince Paramilitary Group, 1994"
Author Photo: Copyright © M.J. Fievre, 2013

First Edition
ISBN: 978-1-940761-18-3

"M.J. Fievre has written a heartfelt and deeply honest coming of age memoir that examines her family as well as her country. We see a girl lose her innocence and her country even as she triumphs through the magic and power of words. *A Sky the Color of Chaos* is a brave and beautiful book from a prodigious talent. It is also a welcomed revelation of a very talented writer's beginnings."

— Edwidge Danticat,
author of *Brother, I'm Dying* and *Breath, Eyes, Memory*

"I'll tell you what's so good about *A Sky the Color of Chaos*, what distinguishes it from the long catalogue of navel-gazing memoirs lining our bookstore shelves. It is an unsparing, honest, and unsentimental evocation of a young woman's struggle for independence amidst the chaos and violence of a nation coming apart at its seams. M.J. Fievre takes us behind her family's closed doors and beyond the security fences and the armed guards, the protests, the murders, and the nightly eruption of gunfire. This is a harrowing personal memoir, friends, and it's an eye on a disturbing chapter in Caribbean history. And it is, ultimately, a triumph."

— John Dufresne,
author of *No Regrets, Coyote*

"M.J. Fievre's powerful memoir *A Sky The Color of Chaos* is a vivid, lyric account of the perils of growing up in Haiti. It brings the headlines to the heart and leaves an indelible mark on the mind."

— Dan Wakefield,
author of *New York in the Fifties*

"M.J. Fievre's fearless and beautifully crafted memoir opens and closes 'beneath the sun's hot glare' in a city from which the author cannot seem to escape. This is a haunting and violent story that runs counter to the more prevailing narrative of strong people elevating themselves above their humble origins. Fievre's brutal and poignantly rendered Port-au-Prince origins had to be left behind, not risen above."

— Johnny Temple,
Editor of *USA Noir: Best of the Akashic Noir Series*

To my father.

one

Port-au-Prince, Haiti—where the sun burned, and the clouds didn't break into rain. Collars melted against necks and Eskimo ice creams melted down hands. Grass withered. Madansara birds fell into parched silence. Taptap and kamyonèt shot by, honking, and the clouds of dust they stirred took hours to settle. Heat rose from the pavement, and windows bottled up that heat.

The old man selling Ibuprophen and Pepto-Bismol from a wheelbarrow in front of Collège Marie Anne complained that he sweated too much, that he chafed, that the insides of his thighs were rubbed raw. The woman standing by the stall of goat and chicken meat hanging from nails in the wood was quick to answer: *She* could feel the sweat run down her back into the crack of her butt, and there was nothing worse.

"Turn on the damn fan," someone said, lazy, sweating.

"Electricity's out again," someone answered.

But the one who'd asked was no longer listening—a soft torpor had crept over him and he fell asleep on the balcony, his cheeks gone slack. Air softly wobbled out of his mouth when he breathed.

On Christ-Roi Street, people stayed on their balconies—women in thin muumuus, men shirtless. Inside, the heat closed in on us—no one could take the overstuffed chairs, the throw rugs, the floors that smelled of Pine-Sol® or Floralin®. The neighborhood swam with squeals, and the never-ending babble became ripples of heat too. The maids were dizzy and the maîtresses de maison frowned and shouted hot Creole words whenever the dust floated, gathered, settled. Whenever heaps of dirty socks and guayabera shirts accumulated in the woven laundry baskets. Whenever toothpaste-water drained slowly.

Christ-Roi is French for Christ, the King, but it was so hot on that street it sometimes felt like Hell had broken loose and come nestling with the inhabitants. Lucifer illuminated the Vacancy sign so his two best friends—lust and insanity—could crash the party. The mini-skirts were shorter on Christ-Roi because even as darkness fell, sticky heat smothered the place. The stifling heaviness of hot, motionless air tantalized the senses, brought a burning fury in you, a semi-delirium.

Tempers flared.

Our neighbor, Mr. Maxwell, ran after his wife with a rawhide in his hand. He grabbed her by the arm and tore her sleeve all the way to the elbow. "Damn you!" he yelled, arms big and hairy, his mouth a thin, bitter line.

When Mrs. Maxwell's husband left for a woman in a mini-skirt, she played Konpa records so loud I couldn't concentrate on my French grammar lessons after school.

That same week, Christ Mon Roi, the bòlèt—lottery—store on Rue Acacia, closed. The owner, Monsieur Corneille, had been robbed at gunpoint and locked in the bathroom.

"I'm moving out of this place," Monsieur Corneille told Papa. "It's so hot I can't but imagine the fires of hell. I see the flames reaching skyward like souls of the dead."

On Christ-Roi Street, the sharp crack of gunfire broke the dusk. Screams sometimes followed, but that night all was quiet. In the kitchen, a cloud of mosquitoes came to hang in front of my eyes. I waved them away; they reappeared a heartbeat later—more brazen. The kitchen was so warm with the smell of cornmeal porridge that Felicie, our femme à tout faire (housekeeper), threw open the window above the sink. She was a broad, square-hipped woman with tough fingers and thick nails. She dressed in loose, floral prints. In the candlelight, she was quiet, going about her work as if afraid to rattle a pot or pan or clank one dish against another. She was sanitizing countertops and applying a high sheen to every inch of stainless steel when Papa made a stormy entrance.

Outside—another gunshot.

Papa's eyebrows joined together in a frown across his forehead. His face was stern, his lips latched tight, and the black-rimmed glasses magnified furious, incisive eyes that held focus above the lens. I knew that face from every angle: He was in one of his moods. I had grown skillful at reading the many browns of Papa's eyes, and the slight changes of his voice. One moment, my father was normal, composed, in control, reliable; the next he was unglued—a wild-eyed stranger, screaming so loud that my ears stung. His face had become my barometer, my instrument for peace. Outside, the rat-tat-tat and the pup-pup-pup of the machine guns continued. The battery-powered TV was on— something about Lt. Gen. Prosper Avril[1] maybe resigning soon as our president. It was 1989. I was eight years old.

"I don't think there'll be school tomorrow," Felicie said.

"What do you know?" Papa asked, his lips pursed, and looking grim.

"I'm going to ask Madame if I should get the lunch bags ready in the morning," Felicie insisted.

Papa was an important man in a suit—a lawyer who left the house early in the morning and came back in the evening, tired, just like that night. He was elegant and sophisticated—tall, athletic, perfect teeth and a robust complexion. There was a drive about him that made his gestures proper and efficient. He carried a chunky leather briefcase with a combination code lock and the latches snapped open. I peeked inside: files, papers, pencils, ink pens, and cheap Bic pens. He removed documents and replaced them in another pocket. As he sorted the contents, he leafed through the pages and mumbled to himself. He finally shut the lid, snapped fast the locks and spun the code wheels.

After supper, as I walked through the kitchen, Papa grabbed my shoulder in his huge hand and yanked my dirty white uniform shirt to speed me up. I stopped because I didn't understand, and he shouted, "Out of my way, Jessica!" A pinprick of spit hit my cheek when he shouted.

Papa's mean look—oh, how much it hurt.

I ran into the bathroom where the carpet was shaggy and damp, the cut-to-fit kind, jammed up against the tub, the one with no running water. Mother was in the kitchen now too—slamming drawers and cabinets. When she got tired of Papa's moodiness, she had a way of making the cupboard do the cursing for her.

---

1   They say that Lt. Gen. Prosper Avril was a trusted member of President François "Papa Doc" Duvalier's Presidential Guard; he was also an advisor and confidante to Jean-Claude "Baby Doc" Duvalier, although their relationship wasn't always smooth. Nicknamed "the Intelligent Prosper Avril" by Papa Doc, he graduated Valedictorian from Haiti's Military Academy; Papa Doc later closed the school for being a hot bed of sedition. Avril was regarded as the "Sphinx" of Haitian politics, a key behind-the-scenes figure in a succession of governments after nationwide riots forced Baby Doc into exile on February 7, 1986. First, he assisted Henri Namphy ("Tiblan" or "Chouchou du peuple") in the June 1988 bloodless coup that overthrew Lesly Manigat. In September of that same year, he overthrew Namphy, his former ally, putting himself as de-facto president to "save the county from anarchy and chaos" and "restore civil and press liberties." He's described by some as charming, "the most honest man in the army," and by others as a manipulator, a "wheeler-dealer," and a "particular corrupt figure in the heyday of the [Duvalier] regime." All agree, however, that he was a shrewd, crafty man.

I sat in the darkness of the bathroom until Mother came to fetch me and said, "Bedtime."

In the bedroom, spooned against my older sister Sœur's back, I looked out the window, as the light of stars sent this way several billion years ago fell softly on my face. In the night, birds cried for lost nests—their voices a foreign thing. Others, I imagined, nestled against each other to warm their wings and forget the day behind them.

Finally the birds quieted down.

Finally: silence.

I learned how expansive silence can be, how forgiving.

It was still dark when I woke up, and Papa was in a rage.

"Open the door," he said. His voice sounded like paper, throats tearing.

Mother, Sœur and I were huddled in the moonlit bedroom I shared with my sister. They'd locked the door.

Pound. Pound. Pound.

Sœur put her hands over her ears. In spite of her stillness, she was restless. My mother begged Papa—through the door—to calm down. The pounding stopped for a few minutes and then began again. "Open up, Mima, or so help me God, I'll break the door down. Mima!"

The name seemed to belong to someone else, even though it was Papa's voice calling Mother. An angry voice—gravelly, loud, insistent. My nerves twitched in the frantic air.

Mother sat on the edge of my bed, bare feet on the tile floor, nightgown twisted around her knees. "Go away, Goule!" She covered the Virgin Mary pendant at her throat with one hand as she spoke his pet name. Her movements were crisp, not muddled by recent sleep. She grimaced when she touched her naked shoulder, and the light skin was turning several different colors.

I was afraid the door would break down.

I couldn't say what had started the trouble with Papa that night, anymore than I could pinpoint the catalyst on any other occasion, but it was likely something simple. He was still out there. He was back to calling her name. "Mima. Mima. Let me in. Let. Me. In."

Pound. Pound. Pound.

He rattled the doorknob with one hand and banged at the wood with the other. The floor was going to swallow me. The bedroom walls started caving in. I imagined dark creatures from the corners of the room—they bobbed their huge heads as they weaved and glided closer.

"I'm going to kill you all," Papa said, and I could feel the rumble of his words in my belly.

Mother kept her hand on my shoulder like a vise. A tear rolled down the silhouette of her shadowed cheek. Her leg was pressed into mine and she bounced it up and down; she stopped when she realized she was doing it, then forgot and started again. Now Sœur was scratching at mosquito bites that were already bloody and raw. She puckered her lips and exhaled a long breath, the way someone does when smoking a cigarette.

"Maman?" I said, touching her hand, and the sound of my own puny voice against all her silence magnified my fear. I reminded myself that night becomes morning.

Mother rubbed her face and turned to look at me. "I bet I look a mess," she said. Her voice had shifted to a higher, strained octave. Her eyes angled up to keep the tears from spilling over.

"You're still pretty," I whispered. I held her arm. She felt rigid and fragile at the same time and I was afraid if I let go, she would topple forward and shatter like glass. "Even with snot on your nose."

"Oh, Jessica, honey," she said, her face damp against my cheeks. Her fingers stroke my head. I could feel my lungs inside my ribs, pushing up and sucking back down.

I often wished Papa gone. That night, I wished a bus would mow him down the next day. I wished for something like a car accident. Something sudden, painless, and unexpected, as though God himself had reached down and rubbed my father out of existence with his godly eraser. What a blessing it would be to have him out of my life, gone, and to know it wasn't my fault. In Haiti, death was near and never new, but I had never courted it in this way.

The sharp crack of gunfire broke the night, the echoes crashing through the rooms of my skull. Rat-tat-tat. Louder than before. Clearer.

Fear washed through me—a reckless electricity. I'd never heard gunshots so close before. I sweated, mostly on my upper lip, the palms of my hands.

Rat-tat-tat.

"It's the neighbors'," Sœur said, breathing through her teeth. She peeked behind the curtains of the window that opened on Christ-Roi Street. "There are men with shotguns."

Pup-pup. Rat-tat-tat. Pound. Pound. Pound.

"Zenglendos," Sœur whispered. Bandits. She looked at the dusty road outside—narrow and deep and tortuous, with lengthening shadows, undergarments and sheets hung out to dry on their sides. "They're breaking into Max Corneille's house."

Papa screamed and smashed things in the living room. Then he was behind the door again. "Open up," he shouted. The doorknob turned clockwise, rattled, and quickly turned counter-clockwise.

"Jessica, help out!"

In her panic, Mother's tongue caught on the S and spit sprayed my cheek. The C in my name was throaty, husky. Mother wedged a chair under the doorknob. She and I leaned with all our might against the door.

Rat-tat-tat. Pup-pup. Pound.

Mother and I were losing the battle. There were only two of us (Sœur was too terrified, too mesmerized by the zenglendos[2] outside), and an angry man was pushing the door from the other side. Papa threw his body weight into a running tackle that started at the other end of the hallway and ended with a splintering kablam at the bedroom door.

The door collapsed inward, sending Mother and me sprawling, crashing the chair into the wall. My temple pulsed in and out.

Rat-tat-tat.

Papa looked at Mother for a long second. I held my breath. Mother's eyes came in his direction but focused on the wall behind him. Her breath was a hollow rasp, almost silent.

Papa grabbed her elbow and leaned in close to her ear. "I told you to open the door." His hands had soft tremors.

She wrestled her arm free and stepped back. "What do you want from me?"

Rat-tat-tat.

I waited for his fist to ball up, for his arm to draw back, but his eyes went dead and he walked to the window, shoving Sœur aside. He looked outside. "One man down," he said. "Max is holding the fort." He swung around. "Sœur, call the police—the number is on the counter." His eyes squinted, narrow and mean.

Sœur didn't move, defiant. Papa wrinkled his lip. He stepped forward, opened his mouth.

"I'll call," I said.

I got up and stood by Sœur. She didn't look at me.

---

2   "Zenglendo" means burglar, bandit, or any kind of violent criminal. The term, reportedly coined by radio news anchor Sonny Bastien, became very popular during the first waves of political terror and violent crime following the dissolution of the Macoutes, the ruthless corps that served as the eyes, ears, and fists of the Duvalier dictatorship. Some say that the word derives from the Haitian-Creole word *zenglen*, which means chips, fragments, or shards of glass (often found after an act of Zenglendism). Others report that "les Zenglens" were the secret police of 19th-century Haitian emperor Faustin Soulouque (1847-1858), who inspired Duvalier to form his Macoutes. In this case, zenglendo connotes more than just a criminal, but rather a thug with a political tinge. Many zenglendos were supposedly former Macoutes, soldiers, or death squad gunmen.

As if on cue, there was the muzzled ring of the telephone outside. Papa spun away, and away from us, turning and raveling the air, each of his steps squeezing my throat tighter. Fear had found its way through my fractured layers.

I helped Mother get on her feet. I hugged her, sticking to her like flesh on a rib. Her face looked drained and dehydrated.

Papa yelled on the phone in the kitchen. "Who's this? Yes, we can hear the gunshots."

His voice softened. And just like that, he seemed over his anger. This was usually the way the rage ended: Papa either burned himself out or something random derailed him. My relief was jumbled with fear and sorrow and, somehow, guilt too.

"Listen, I have to get off and call the police." Pause. "Zenglendos, apparently." He kept his voice steady and neutral, making it hard to tell what he was thinking.

Rat-tat-tat.

Papa was off the phone: He paced from door to window, from room to room, checking on locks and latches. He wore a stranger's face—tight, unreadable. Sœur, Mother, and I were at the window, a pyramid of huddled grog and apprehension. Iron bars kept out the terrifying zenglendos.

Rat-tat-tat. Police sirens blared in the distance. Tires squealed. A woman screamed. Dogs—barking at the bone-white moon, the heat, the dark, the commotion, each other. Their barking—shards of glass I pictured scraping the inside of my head. Shards bleeding out my ears, polished and colored.

"Do you see the fireflies?" Sœur asked, her attention shifting from the police cars. She pointed outside the window, her voice a reverent whisper.

When I think about that night, I can't remember the stars, or the shape of the moon's face. But the fireflies flared haltingly, and I could see the outlines of the garden shadowed by dark trees, their branches tangled like a woman's hair after love—or battle. When the sun rose in the morning, and shone on the garden, the flowers would light up—daisies, black-eyed Susans, hibiscus choublak. A bird made its call, two quick dips followed by a line of maniacal laughter.

Rat-tat-tat. Rat-tat-tat. Again—hours later.

The darkness was thinning above the mountains, but night still pooled in the trees and rat holes. Sleep-sodden and crusty-eyed, I got out of bed to stand behind the iron bars of the window; the roosters still snoozed, and the sun was in hiding behind the hills and the shacks that peppered these hills.

Another gunshot—pop—sharp, insistent.

I made out the angular profile of Sœur, still asleep in the twin bed in her pink pajamas. I whispered, "Sœur, did you hear?"

She snored rhythmically, her mouth slightly open. She had fallen asleep reading and her glasses were trying to get away from her face. She'd folded her hands on her chest like a corpse. Her breathing was as soothing a sound as I'd ever heard, but it wouldn't lull me back to sleep.

Another gunshot—pop—followed by a rooster's quack.

At first, I was unable to dive into the darkness, afraid of every shape, every shadow. Then, I found my way toward my parents' bedroom, hands extended in front of me, small step after small step, mosquitoes nibbling my earlobes. The dark made it harder to stumble to the bed unscathed, but I made it with just a stubbed toe. My parents' door was ajar, and in the moonlight I could see the vanity, the chest of drawers, and the padded chair. Jeweled chopsticks and flowered pins laid scattered on the vanity top.

Papa wasn't snoring, nor was he shouting in his sleep. He slept with a smile, as if remembering a saint, one he knew personally, one he took personally. My mother wore a sleeveless muumuu showing off her supple biceps. I looked at her soft profile, at the bubble of black hairnet swelling her head. I put my forefinger under her nose to feel for breath. Still alive.

"Réveillez-vous," I whispered. "Wake up. They're shooting again."

Mother moaned when I bounced the mattress. She opened her eyes—but only for a moment. She stretched her legs out. Her body creaked, or maybe it was the bed.

"Come here," my father said. He swallowed several times, and his Adam's apple bobbed under the skin of his throat.

When I opened my mouth, butterflies escaped from my throat. "I… Huh…" My spine tingled. My brain buzzed with bees. I hesitated, reading Papa's face to find out whether he was in a dangerous, quiet rage that would hang on to him. Finally, I slid between the two warm and soft bodies, into the humid comfort of the occupied bed, thinking for a moment that my parents were beautiful. Papa was handsome and successful and rarely home; Mother was witty and tender. His voice boomed; hers tinkled like tiny bells.

"You should be used to this, Jessica," Papa said after the next clatter of rat-tat-tat. He asked, "Est-ce que tu aimes ton papa?" ("Do you love your papa?") He scratched his left palm with his right fingers, making a papery sound because his skin was dry. The alarm clock ticked out each second, uncoiling the minutes like a maddened snake poised to strike.

I touched Papa's palms and his fingers weaved into mine; his fingertips circled me, recaptured me from the night. "I love you," I said. I leaned into his armpit, my face against his chest, against the beating hum of him, and I smelled his skin, a non-scent really.

Rat-tat-tat.

My father once said Port-au-Prince was a city of upheavals and kraze zo— destructions. The storms around the city broke forth without warning and without vindication.[3]

Papa belonged there.

Outside, the sky was a chemistry of perfect shadows—a tomb in which people buried their lies.

---

3   According to the *Sun Sentinel*, critics decried the arrests, beatings, banishments, and state of siege during the government of Lt. Gen. Prosper Avril, as the violence seemed to indicate that Haiti's ruler planned to turn his regime into a dictatorship and renege on promises to hold elections. I often imagine armed men combing a neighborhood. I imagine time stopping—a bullet hanging in the air, a vapor trail behind it. The bullet suspended like a large eye. Then: someone crumbling into the pavement, falling sideways.

two

In the morning, Bòsfàn, the carpenter, came. Sœur and I watched him at work—watched the way he swung the hammer against the doorframe, pounding the nail into the wood in one blow. The carpenter's face glowed in the light of the kerosene lamp, which was smudged, like the gauze of ash that grows over embers. I asked Bòsfàn about his lips, about his cheek—bloody, swollen. He said the mob had beaten him on his way to the Boulangerie du Quartier.[4] His roughened hands took the tools in a firm grip and glided smoothly over the wood.

His nostrils flared. "Luckily, one of the men realized I wasn't the macoute[5] they were looking for." He looked away from the broken door. A few hairs stood in the line between his neck and sagging chin. "What happened *here?*" His jaw clenched.

"Zenglendos," Sœur said.

We were not to talk about Papa's fits of rage.

On the balcony, a vertigo buzz of insects rose and fell in the heat, and the air was thick as a towel over our mouths. On the sidewalk, a woman was

---

4   Government critic Hubert DeRoncerey denounced Lt. Gen. Prosper Avril's "regime of terror." The violence targeted the opposition but also had strong repercussions on the lives of average Joes (like Bòsfàn). According to the *Daily Gazette*, DeRoncerey was kicked, clubbed with guns, and had a cigarette jammed in his eye. Avril was said to have ordered the arrest and exile of several prominent opposition politicians, sparking public anger that ultimately drove him from the country.

5   Haitians named Duvalier's secret police force after the mythological Tonton Macoute (Uncle Gunnysack) bogeyman who kidnaps and punishes unruly children by snaring them in a gunnysack (macoute) and carrying them off to be consumed at breakfast.

saying, "He broke my back in two places." These words were like bird cries that cluttered the air for a moment, then died.

On Christ-Roi Street, the afternoon was noisy with Bob Marley reggae. A girl in a golden evening jacket fried griyo in a pot of oil over a tiny fire; another baked jumbles of tablèt out of brown sugar and shredded coconut. The street vendors—almost all women—had their spots staked out on the side of the street: someone's tòtòt or fransik mangoes; someone else's true "Kentucky" fried chicken. The wind teetered trashcans. Rats ran along the telephone lines; chickens squawked and pecked the concrete ground's cracks.

I watched the ice-cream man with his red cap and the gray sheets of the newspapers in the hands of passers-by. The woman parking her red car in front of our fence was my aunt, my matant.

Soon, Mother and her sister were talking in the kitchen. Mother was still in her linen suit, back from her eight-to-four job as a clearing officer at the Banque Nationale. Matant's hair was in a bun; she'd spent the day at the state hospital, where she was on duty as an anesthesiologist. They were alone—Papa was at work, Sœur in the bedroom, reading, listening to George Michael.

Their conversation rolled back and forth like a soccer ball. They were good at this. They'd been having kitchen-table talks for years. They knew when to interject, when to change the topic, when to sit quietly and nod. Their words trickled by me, nothing more than background static, like the continuous hum of the fan, now that the electricity was back. I was not aware that I was listening until the words that casually tumbled out onto the kitchen table began to break my heart: *I can't leave him.*

"He will fight for the girls," Mother said. Pink rollers now inflated her head size.

She was lonely inside—I could see it in the tilt of her head. I wondered if she thought about kicking and screaming sometimes.

Mother told her sister stories about my father. She used the words *prowess* with women, *untrustworthiness*, and *obscure delinquencies.* I needed an excuse to hear the conversation clearly so I walked into the kitchen, pulled a Spur from the fridge and held the lukewarm bottle against my forehead. Condensation mixed with sweat and ran down my face. I squatted and rubbed my hands on my jeans. My t-shirt stuck to my chest and back, and if I tried, I could smell myself. A comforting smell.

"We were happy," Mother said. "Those days were good days, and if someone would have told me they would end, I would have told them they were fools."

Matant scoffed. "Time changes stone, no matter what you do."

The clock in the kitchen ticked, clicking off each second with a jump. Time goes slower when the second hand jerks instead of sweeping smoothly. The hour hand crept toward five.

"Jessica, go back to the balcony," Mother said. "Granmoun ap pale." It's grown-up talk.

Her face was dark, her breath rasping. A pimple flourished above her eyebrow. "Yes, Ma'am."

Back on the balcony, I watched a herd of boys on bikes pedal into view. They were shirtless, sailing down the street in careless whooshing speed. Junior, Mendel and the other neighborhood boys played barefoot in the long and narrow street. When it got unbearably hot, they grabbed their soccer balls and took their loud jokes into the shadows of the alley. They laughed, giggled and shouted, and the sounds of their rolling voices bounced off the walls of our house and blended with the low hum of the Caribbean city.

But I was no longer paying attention to the boys. Something was going on—down there.

Junior and his gang flew away when an angry mob gathered in the street, yelling, "Long live the President!" They shoved a man whose body was covered with wounds, bruises and blood. They held his legs and arms down.

Before I could say, "Jésus, Marie, Joseph," flames were licking his body and clothes with their burning tongues. *Oh, the pretty colors*, I thought before my brain registered the man was screaming, jerking with flames that stripped flesh from his hands. My fascination changed into something else, sank lower in my stomach. As the man stretched his neck, he wept and twitched, and I imagined his skin crackling from the heat, the fire sucking the oxygen out of his lungs to help feed his inferno. Sweat grew crystals across my brows and upper lip as the man's hair shriveled and tore away. In my belly there was a chemical burn, stomach acid on smooth, pink muscle. My heart escalated its rate and pressure to where it pulsed in my ears.

From the balcony, I couldn't see all of it, but I knew his muscles were melting. Bones cracked in the heat, brains broiled in his skull. He soon was a pile of dark gray ashes next to sewage washing through the shacks. His clothes burned and smoldered around the bare, erupted flesh of his back.

My hands jumped in their skins. On the balcony, I gasped, throbbing and covered in sweat. A weak sob leaked from me. I then became aware of another warm, living body next to mine. My mother hugged me. A sick feeling scrabbled up my throat.

The man's skin was gone. From his hands, his arms, his chest. His shirt had melted into him, taking skin with it as it dripped onto the ground.

"Popular justice," my mother murmured. "They kill the macoutes."

Matant rushed us in. "You shouldn't be watching," she said.

I never learned who this man was. They didn't reveal his name on the news that night, but they did mention he was one of Baby Doc's spies—a macoute.[6] In front of the battery-powered TV in the living room, I sat on my father's knee. Papa, exhausted and inexhaustible all at once, made a clicking noise and moved his legs up and down, his body askew as if pulled in all directions. I was a machann on her donkey, bouncing into the air, battling the rugged terrain. The man on the screen said that, because of the violence in Haiti, many families sought a safe haven overseas.

"I worried about you," I said to Papa. "You were not home, and the mob was outside." It was true. I no longer wanted him dead.

Papa smiled and watched me with the dark eyes of a forest animal. "You love your papa, don't you, girl?"

When I asked him about the macoutes, Papa told me about the night he ventured in the streets of Port-au-Prince, hours after the government-imposed curfew, when, years ago, my uncle André had been arrested at the airport in a case of mistaken identity.

"The macoutes took him to the Casernes, behind the National Palace." Papa stretched out certain words, making them sound like the most important words I would ever hear.

I watched his face, the lines that formed between his brows. "He would have been transferred to Fort Dimanche and been killed there," he said.

But one of Papa's students at the Faculty of Law and Economic Sciences was a haut-gradé in the army and a close friend of Baby Doc. His name was Colonel Ismael. "I knew he lived on Malval Street in Turgeau, but didn't know which house was his."

It was already seven o'clock when my parents parked the car on the side of the road in Turgeau, in the blackout of the city—no streetlights, stoplights, car lights, driving at night illegal. No lights in houses but candles. At any moment, a patrol car could emerge from the bowels of the night and heavily armed men arrest them. Nonetheless, they went from house to house, yelling, "Ismael! Ismael!"

---

6   The Macoutes were Duvalier's dreaded goon squads—his private militia. According to the *Sun Sentinel*, "crowds of the same people they had beaten, tortured, extorted, and killed, were clamoring for their blood and hunting them down in alleys, side streets and houses. Stories and eyewitness accounts mentioned Macoutes corpses burned, mutilated, beheaded, and put on display."

"Ou kwè se pa kay sa a?" Mother said. "Maybe this house over there?" My mother's shoes, a pair of strappy sandals, slapped over the sidewalk.

My father—resourceful, invested in helping his brother-in-law, called Ismael's name in the night, until a woman came out on the balcony, her hard, thin legs and arms looking wired onto her, like a puppet's. "Who's asking for Ismael?" she demanded.

Because of my father's determination, Uncle André was saved.

I imagined Colonel Ismael, his tightly trimmed mustache and tasseled loafers. The circles under his eyes were stained. Papa was good at telling stories— he had a repertoire and knew the right cues and markers, when to include dialogue and when to hurry the plot, when to paint a scene or salt a detail. He seemed to tell the story the same way each time, but if I were to compare the latest telling with an earlier one, I was sure to uncover refinements.

I leaned against Papa and breathed, arms wrapped around his pants, a tipped cheek resting on his knee. I was lost in the tale of Uncle André and Colonel Ismael—until my backbone didn't tingle and my heart beat its normal rhythm, until my sides felt as composed as my face, wiped of its bewildered expression, until my hands no longer trembled and my knees were stable.

Papa let me watch Languichatte's comedy hour 'til late. Alone on the carpet, I was surrounded by candles; the electricity came and went, came and went. We scheduled our days around the expectation that power would be cut off at some point. The house had come to smell of kerosene and sulfur and coffee and the thick peanut butter we ate at breakfast on our toast. When the power went out, cries rolled down the streets, "Yo pran li! Yo pran li!" followed by the fumbling for matches to light candles and oil lamps, which brought a haunted glow to everything. Objects became sinister, political anecdotes terrifyingly real, with macoutes and zenglendos lurking beyond the comfort of the swaying flames.

The hot dry air coming from Christ-Roi Street pushed on my neck and bare arms. I drew the canvas curtains. The room darkened, but the mirror on the wall still reflected a crescent moon. I struck a match and took in the sweet sulfur smell. *How does it feel to be burned alive?* I liked that my fingers could make such a thing as fire happen. I liked that fire could make a square of paper towel look like the American highways on television, with tiny fire-colored cars scurrying around. I liked the sound and even more the smell of human hair, of *my* hair burning when I put the flame close to my braids.

Saturday, the day after the burning, Felicie brought water in a recycled paint bucket to the bathroom.[7] She helped me undress. I shed my clothes like scales and slithered into the aluminum basin kept in the bathtub; it was so big I could lie in it. Some water splashed out onto the smudged tile.

"I hear you saw a man burning," Felicie said.

She filled the basin with fresh basil and tea leaves and added another pot of water that smelled sharply of lavender and something sweeter and subtler, running under the astringent scent of the fèy bwa. She knelt by the tub, stirring a thin stream of cooler water from the bucket into the mix.

"I did see him," I said. I remembered the flames catching in his hair and his clothes; I imagined the scent of burning flesh.

Felicie's face was scribbled, a thousand wrinkles swimming in every direction. Under her headscarf, gray hair piled on her head in stiff curls. Felicie babbled endlessly—words strung together like a macaroni necklace. And she fidgeted.

"Was he a bad man?" I asked.

"I don't know." Felicie's head was tilted to one side.

They'd said on T.V. that he'd been a macoute, but Papa said that, really, he could have been anybody—in the wrong place, at the wrong time.

The water was too cold to bear at first, but quickly became invigorating. Felicie's hands, slick with soap, passed over my arms and shoulders. She was scrubbing my back with a rough sponge when Papa stepped into the bathroom in a fluid rush. A path of Bien-être cologne followed him like a tail of smoke.

"Jessica, have you been through my music records?" he asked with an edge in his voice, his face contorted by curses.

Papa paced back and forth, his eyes hard between down-drawn brows. A leather belt, the edges cracked, clasped around my father's waist like a black snake. Papa had never used a martinette or rigoise to discipline us. He preferred the belt.

My throat burned—as if I had swallowed a small piece of glass.

"You went through my records and Nana Mouscouri is missing," he said.

His hair was wild. It stood on end. He rubbed his eyes with the back of his fist, and then pointed his finger toward me. "*You* went through my records. Do you know what they do to thieves?" He paused to give more weight to his words, as my heart squawked. "They burn their right hands." His mouth twisted.

---

7   In 1964 the government of Papa Doc created CAMEP, the *Centrale Autonome Métropolitaine d'Eau Potable*, responsible for supplying water the Port-au-Prince metropolitan area. The water company did not provide water 24/7. Rainwater was collected in "bokit" (buckets) whenever provided, stored in plastic containers in the backyard or outdoor kitchen, and brought inside when needed. The water business is still huge in Haiti, as people who can afford it buy truckloads of water to fill water tanks. Big trucks carry the water to the private houses.

There was a heaviness in his voice. When he unbuckled his belt and snapped it from the loops, I hunched down. And although I squeezed my eyes closed, his face remained in the back of my eyelids. Felicie continued the circular movement of the sponge on my back, as if the ceiling wasn't about to fall on my head.

"I didn't do it," I said, exposed in my nakedness.

I opened my eyes and tried to win him over with honesty, even though I was lying. Shame, I knew, speckled my cheeks. Led by some sort of fascination for everything that was *him* (his glasses, a half-dozen watches, old photographs), I had gone through his records, trying to glean something new about his life. I might have misplaced the missing record.

I stared into the air with damp, unblinking eyes. Papa's words slipped past my ears, down my shrinking body, over my bowl-shaped knees. I heard him and smelled him and saw him, but I was quiet.

"Do you want me to burn your hand?" he asked.

I looked around at the shelves of folded white towels, the glass cupboard with its vials of secret remedies—lwil maskriti, iodine, sodium bicarbonate, a box of green clay from Source Puante. I expected the fury of swift justice—my father's belt on my bare skin. But Mother's voice snaked through the hallway.

"Goule," she cried. "I found it."

Papa removed his glasses, wiped them on the collar of his business shirt. His eyes tightened; faint lines like spider webs radiated from his mouth and I wanted to trace them with my fingertips. As he walked away, I could still feel the weight of his eyes, lines etched around them too.

Felicie unplugged the drain. Then she dipped the sponge in a pitcher. Starting at my shoulders, she squeezed the sponge, forcing warm water to rinse the soap off of my body—this current of flares. She dried me with a soft towel, massaging my body from head to toe. I could feel the firm, warm weight of her hands through the towel, as their vigorous rubbing jogged my head gently back and forth.

I was trembling.

"Your mother warned you about this," she said. "You're always touching his stuff."

"Did you hear? He wanted to burn my hand."

Somewhere, on Christ-Roi Street, someone pulled a trigger, and the bullets soared up, their explosions trembling through our throats.

The slam of the car door in the afternoon meant my father was loosening his necktie with a free hand as he walked toward the house. Then he was up the stairs and in the living room. Keys jingled in the multitude of locks, the sounds muffled under the peal of Mother's laughter. The door of my room opened wide, and his shadowy form filled the doorway.

"Ready for some couscous?" he asked. He was no longer upset, but he wasn't smiling. He was not stern, exactly, but not open either. No particular emotion tilted his features, and this scared me more than his anger—a small fear, just a pang, brief as a paper cut.

I nodded, and while Papa took out pots and pans, I stood by the kerosene stove and watched Felicie wash down the refrigerator; it was leaking because of the recurring power cuts. I leaned down as Papa minced garlic and wished I could tell him how his couscous smelled yummy but tasted like wet toilet paper. He made us what he called "gourmet meals" at least once a week, and I kept up a constant stream of *oohs* and *ahs* and compliments, which sounded so exaggerated that Papa raised an eyebrow and suspected me of mockery.

He bent over the food in the skillet. He pinched salt between his fingers and dashed it in. He paid attention, deeply, to the textures and colors and smells, and a smile formed upon his lips.

"Here, try this," he said, lifting a spoon of couscous.

I tried not to cringe. We had bolero music on in the background, and it was another one of those long, slow, lazy afternoons—the sun didn't burn through the clouds; the clouds didn't break into rain. Papa was annoyed with Mother, who checked to make sure the stove wasn't leaking gas and told him he forgot to talk to the landlord about putting some more locks and latches on the doors. Felicie did dishes behind us, in a futile attempt to keep the kitchen clean. As Papa plated up our food, his face widened with excitement, because I was going to love this food he had made with his hands. I slammed my fork into the couscous and it was half-cooked. The kitchen had a greasy smell.

I said, "Oh, man, this is good," and that was the highest praise. "This is good."

And he believed me. He said his couscous had a twist of culinary adventure—rich and memorable.

When Papa went to the balcony for a nap behind the large hibiscus plant, Mother granted me permission to throw away my meal. Papa slept better during the day because he was haunted. Night haunted. And when the spooky things came—memories of his own childhood—he haunted my mother. He woke her up and told her his nightmares, to pull her into his suffering, to taunt her into saving him.

The radio hissed and burst into snatches of chatter in Creole. Mother made sandwiches. Sœur and I picked the vegetables off and ate quickly, eyeing each other competitively, mouths bulging. We peeled oranges for the slow rip of the flesh in our thumbs, the sweet dotting of our noses with juice. We sucked the threads of each fruit, laughing. Sweat rolled down my ribs as I poured a cup of Spur from a glass bottle in the fridge.

"Don't wake him up," Mother said, her eyes lazy and mellow, bored. She stood in front of the sink and let the cold water from the pitcher run on her small hands. She dried her hands on her apron. "You know how he gets—"

She was interrupted by the neighborhood's roar of shrieks and giggles. Yo bay li! Yo bay li! The electricity was back. I adjusted the fan, raised my arms and let the dry air blow across me.

When Papa woke up, he was in a good mood. "We're going to get ice cream," he said with a smile, tossing his car keys from his right hand to his left.

He exuded a scent part sun, part sweat, and all him. I put on my favorite shirt, one with a peace sign on it. Mother stood on the balcony, white patent leather sandals and toes curled to the edge of the concrete. Our dog Pipo had broken his collar and gotten into the house; he jumped up and down as if on a trampoline.

"Are you coming?" I asked Mother.

She said no and blew a giant achoo, her white eyelet dress billowing in the wind. I whispered, "A tes souhaits," but she didn't hear me, busy spitting the devil out. I hopped in the car with Sœur.

The moon, about to rise, gave the sky an expectant glow. In the front seat, Papa drove without a word and Sœur dozed against the window glass next to him. On the radio, they said the nightly shootings were getting worse in Port-au-Prince. The current president, Lt. Gen. Prosper Avril, might be leaving the Palais National. He hadn't even been president for two years. Papa didn't seem to care one way or another. *Same old nonsense*, he mumbled. The road tossed the Audi from one side to the other.

We passed a beggar on folded knee; one glance created a flimsy bond, frail as a spider web that broke as we drove away. Stray dogs dug on piles of ashy trash on which ragged children played. One kid slipped a finger in his mouth and whistled until the heat of Port-au-Prince took his breath away. Another shouted at us, but his words were snatched away by the hot air, sucked up in the fury of my father's driving. Other sounds reached us: a mother calling her pitit home for dinner, the mew of a hungry cat, the long wail of a police siren. I twisted and twirled the same strand of black hair, weaving a pretend dreadlock between my fingers. I kicked my feet against the back of Papa's seat in anticipation for the ice cream.

"Papa is angry," Papa said out of nowhere, turning off the radio. His teeth squeezed his bottom lips. His hands cradled the wheel. The heel of his palm pressed the gear shaft, his knee rising when he engaged the clutch.

He wasn't mad at me. In the car, that night, Papa said he was furious at his dead father. For years, he'd waited for my grandfather to acknowledge and love him—but the man only saw Goule as a pitit deyò, a bastard. When his estranged father visited, Papa spent his days away from home, his only defense a silent defiance, a refusal to engage, what some would call teenage rebellion. In nature, he felt dim and far away from the world and its rumors. Close to something larger than himself, something, he supposed, others would call God.

He kept his eyes on the road. "I said to myself, 'There is no God,' but my body objected. My body knew truth in spite of my brain."

He'd lie in the moss of the bog and watch the moon, filled with hate and self-pity. *Why?* The word barely a whisper swallowed by the wind, a plea for something you can't have. The air moved under its fragile weight. *Why?* A knot of pain throbbed in the back of his neck. He didn't return home at night until the moon was high above the trees, laying a dust of light over everything. In the morning, the new light would be clean, the air fresh, the smell of late summer moving in across the lake, the water cooler.

When Papa was eighteen, his father died. Papa did not go to the funeral. He did not see the man's family wrap him in a cotton sheet and pin his eyelids closed. Papa remembered the lightness in his stomach, as if his body were empty on the inside. He remembered how calm he felt. A coolness passed over his heart and wrapped around it in a perplexing fashion. He knew this feeling for what it was—the cushion of control was eroding, and he was scared sleepless of what would be revealed in its absence. He didn't go to the funeral. He walked past the cemetery at dusk, stray dogs howling at his footfalls. The outdoor market still reeked of animal blood, but there were no more freshly butchered rib-racks hanging on hooks. *The moon is throwing knives through the trees*, he thought, looking up at the sky. And that's the night he became a writer, shaping images and emotions into structured plots. He wrote dozens of stories, and was later published in some fairly respected venues in Saint Marc through his twenties. In his prose, however, he kept a part of himself hidden away. What was really *him* remained folded inward—a secret waiting to reveal itself, a true tale waiting to unwind.

As he told me this, he sounded surprised at the depth of the anger he still harbored, and ashamed of it, too. His face was drained of color. There was a sad, starved look about it, like some small, feral animal, something hunted. We grow up and are lost in time—unhinged. Parts of us trail off, disconnected, filled with longing. Papa was mired in some bleak empty space inside himself where I couldn't follow—a place where personal demons still dwelled. He wished he could be different but, although my grandfather had been dead for thirty years, Papa's mouth was still dirty with rage. I imagined Papa a young man, those epic days, finding himself, verging on success, on failure, his mind gripped by loneliness, his father inside him.

I preferred his other stories, about macoutes and run-away grooms, which made me want to tell stories of my own, to write poems brief as brush strokes, miniature ripples of syllables. Papa's loneliness settled in my chest—a small, hard knot. His sorrow, not completely alien, took me out of myself, made me restless and uneasy. My ears roared with the awkward sound of Papa's gone quiet. I wished Sœur were awake.

As the Audi seesawed down roads slick with mud, garbage smelled pungent and rotten and warm. Outside my window on John Brown Avenue, the trees whizzed past, dark heaps of gray against a darkening sky.

I loved the swirled ice-cream cone on top of the flat-roofed Carvel ice-cream parlor. The owner, Madame Roland, had cat eyes and a laugh that bubbled out of her chest with a gasp if you said something even halfway clever. She threw her head back for dramatic effect, calling attention to her enormous bosom, which had a life independent of Madame Roland's. She stroked my hair affectionately and told me I was pretty. Papa was proud; his eyes were soft and his face broke open like a sapodilla fruit with the brilliant brown meat inside. His face wrinkled in delicate lines along the sides of his mouth. He took Sœur's hand in his, slipped a twenty-five-gourde bill into her palm and folded her fingers over the money so she could pay Madame Roland. A bubble of eagerness rose in my chest.

Sœur's favorite was two scoops of rum raisin. Tongue flicking, she spun on the red stool at the green marble counter, looking at the faded drawings Madame Roland's children posted in the window. I marveled over the strawberry ice cream's smooth coldness on my tongue.

"Isn't it good to have dessert before dinner?" I asked.

"Always," my sister said.

As we crossed the parking lot to get back into the car, tiny rhinestones fell off my shirt, the peace sign crumbling, disappearing. A raspy six-year-old voice followed me in the wind. "Maman, look, I found a diamond, a diamond! Maman, look!"

His face lit up, glowed, beamed. And his chubby fingers coddled the treasure.

Outside the ice-cream parlor, a police officer circled the white Audi, stiff-legged like a chyen peyi wondering where to pee. He wore a filthy uniform with unruly hair sticking up with grease and dirt. His eyes were set far apart and were tilted and dark like a calf's eyes.

He swung his rifle around. "Where are you going?" he asked. It was a voice so rusty I wondered if he'd spoken all day.

"Home," Papa said, his face unreadable.

Officially, there were no more macoutes, although they still existed as a loose political power, supporting certain political figures. Those who had replaced them did not follow a better protocol. Sœur surveyed the man's movements with nervous eyes, as though any unanticipated moves would lead to tragedy. My insides were tightly balled fists.

"Ah," the man with the rifle said, his voice threatening hours of delay, if he liked.

He suddenly recognized my father and the cop's face spread out in glee. "Maître," he said. "Remember me? I was in your Introductory Law class."

He pointed at Papa, "Best teacher I ever had."

Papa was known around the university for his sound disposition and self-composure—a man who moved and gestured with deliberate grace. This other Papa was not real to me, but rather a glorified abstraction, his agitation concealed around his students beneath a smoothed and polished exterior. The Papa I *did* know, I carried around like a dark mass of extra body, a cloak, or a mask.

They talked for a while, the man a tad nostalgic, my father beaming, proud to be acknowledged as a charismatic and brilliant scholar-teacher. I imagined him in front of the old-fashioned blackboard that smelled of chalk dust and showed faintly visible ghosts of previous lectures.

When we got in the car, the officer waved us goodbye.

three

Of my father's childhood, I only knew what Mother told me as she plumped, fluffed, and patted my pillow to prefigure sleep. When I was exhausted by the disquiet, the storms that rose out of nowhere, subsided, made way for others, a story consoled me. And of the few stories Mother told about Papa Goule, the one that stayed with me was about ruined shoes.

On the way to Mr. Jean's store, young Goule looked at his old shoes. The soles were rubbed almost through. The toes were too soft, one of them already split wide open, and several times Goule had lost his footing, landing once on both hands. In vain had the boy tried to save the shoes; adhesive tape didn't hold the sides together long enough for him to take two steps, and glue was far more trouble than it was worth. Besides, his feet had grown over the summer.

He tried to figure out if his mother would be able to afford him new boots. The night before, his father had come to the house, and his parents had argued about money, about his father's *real* family in another town in Saint Marc.

"You're no man," his mother had yelled.

She'd thrown a plate of food on the green painted wall, where it had shattered into a hundred pieces.

Goule had wanted to run to the kitchen and tell them to stop, but he had been afraid. He had stayed in bed, keeping the tears at bay, until he had drifted off to sleep and seen himself soaring through the skies of Saint Marc, over the beautiful mountains.

In the morning, men with machetes cut through mango and avocado trees; they needed the wood for the charcoal. Women balanced large bundles on their heads as they walked toward the market; children trailed along behind.

The earth was red in the morning and Goule thought the sky must have rained rust over the sweeping countryside.

Leaves shuffled. His mother and he walked increasingly narrow roads and past the ruined church, past the cemetery that holds uncles and cousins, grass curving away from the headstone fragments. Papa named the relatives aloud, pointing, correcting himself from time to time.

A tinkling bell announced their visit to the store.

Mr. Jean welcomed them warmly. "Man Simone," he said, "banm ti nouvèl ou."

Goule's mother, face as shiny as an avocado, set her bag down and scanned the racks of sandals, leather shoes and boots. Her eyes worked in an organized, back-and-forth, up-and-down motion.

"These cost all right," she said, pointing at the ugliest pair of shoes. They were green and resembled twin kannòt—fishing boats—more than they did shoes.

"What about those sneakers?" Goule asked.

His mother said he couldn't have them because they cost twice as much.

Mr. Jean asked Goule to take off a shoe. The eight-year-old boy stood on the metal ruler with the stationary heel and sliding toe. Mr. Jean announced he was a size thirteen and said he might have something inexpensive in the back room.

The man disappeared through the curtains heavy with heat and returned carrying a shoe box with a dusty shade of green—a thick cardboard.

The box contained an old pair of shoes. Mr. Jean wiped them off and the burnish of the old polish still gleamed underneath the furry tendrils of dust.

Goule used a horn to ease the shoes onto his feet in front of the mirror. They were not the shape of his feet; his toes curled over and the tips pressed onto the soles.

But he liked them. He took a few steps in front of the mirror, admiring the leather shine.

"How do they feel?" his mother asked.

"Fine. They feel fine. And they look wonderful."

"Are you sure they fit?" she insisted. "They look tight. Do you want to try another size?"

Goule tried to wiggle his toes. The shoes did not fit now, but they would probably expand with time. Anything but the horrible, green twin kannòt.

"No, these are perfect."

"Okay. Let's go."

They had just left when Goule realized that even if the shoes did expand a little, they would never fit. His toes could not move. He hesitated a second. Should he tell his mother? He didn't want her to scold him for wearing impractical shoes he had chosen in a fit of vanity. He was the one who had said the shoes were perfect. Confessing his pain and asking his mother to go back to the store would bring him down. Would Mr. Jean take them back? He could not tell the truth. His mother would want him to be strong and endure the pain. Like a man. *Be a man*, she said to his father.

Waves of heat streamed up from the pavement, scorching the balls of his feet through his thin soles. An ache shot across his arches. Goule's face contorted in a grimace, his teeth grinding, his eyes rolling. His feet numbed, he opted for a smaller, quieter pace, as he hobbled his way to the house.

"Are you sure you're okay?" his mother asked.

Dusty sunrays fell between the leaves and branches of the large, knotted trees. The road was steep, covered in scrabbly and slippery gravel. Soft corns formed between his rubbing toes, as well as blisters under his toenails.

"I am fine."

He counted the clouds. He tried to focus on the rippling and gurgling of the river. The breeze blew and ruffled the smooth surface. Women washed clothes on the bank, beat the dirt out of them with a stick. Goule wished he could take off his shoes and socks, turn up the legs of his pants, and plunge his feet into the water. They ached fiercely with powerful throbs of pain that shot up into his heels and nested there.

They walked under the breadfruit trees. Some branches were thick, others long and slender, foliage clustered at their tips. The leaves were sensual, bright green and glossy on the upper surface, dull and dirty yellow on the underside—a graceful tapestry. His mother would pick the breadfruits that had turned lavender, with their harsh, sandpaper-like rind.

Goule asked if they could sit.

"No time to waste," she said.

The pain brought Goule fear, as he didn't feel in control of his legs. He tried not to bend his knees as he moved forward.

If he could open up to her—

They walked alongside the fields, where the crickets and the bees buzzed. Men with straw hats lifted hay with pitchforks. He looked at his mother with her long rayon skirt. She was a schoolteacher—trim, intelligent, serious, brutal in her way.

They walked together into the kitchen. His mother hung up her handbag in the hall closet and washed the dishes in warm, soap-creamy water.

Goule crawled across the kitchen on his hands and knees. In his room, a cloud of mosquitoes descended upon his flesh. He swatted with one hand and removed his socks and shoes with the other. His bloody feet looked like two swollen hunks of chopped meat, with open sores, the worst blister about the size of a silver dollar.

Goule sat on the floor. He didn't want to be a tough guy anymore. He would not be able to wear these shoes a second time, even if it meant disappointing his mother.

He limped to the kitchen. He would tell her about the pain and his feet looking like overstuffed sausages. He wanted to. He *had* to.

His mother soaked bread in milk, then mashed and mixed it with ground beef and spices. She rolled her boulettes into balls, coated with flour and cheese, and fried them until they turned golden brown.

"Mezanmi! What on earth happened?" his mother asked, looking at his feet, black and purple, shiny and swollen.

Tears streamed down Goule's face.

"The shoes," he stammered. "Maman, they hurt my feet. I can't take it anymore."

His mother gasped. Goule held his breath, waiting for her disappointed glare and her screams. Was she going to threaten him to smash his head just like she had his father?

But she nodded, rubbing his eyes. She gestured him to sit down on a chair, which he did. She grabbed a towel and the bottle of Barbancourt rum to clean up his wounds.

He calmed down, and she held him for a minute, without the two of them saying a word. She caressed his cheek.

"Let's have some boulettes," she said. "We'll get you other shoes later."

He didn't know if he ever felt more alone.

Mother told me stories in a soothing tone that changed into a deeper, growling voice for the lougawou or witches with sharp teeth. She didn't put an end to her chores when plunging into the plot. I wrote her tales in a diary with a blue plastic cover. I let my imagination go wild, filling in the details, the way Mother did when she shared her stories.

four

Papa watched Mother as she clasped her pearl necklace closed. For her birthday, Mother's hair was up in an elaborate bun. Languorous permed curls dangled along the sides of her face. Papa was too far to hold me, and when I reached over to him, he took my hand—for a second or two. Then he let go.

"Remember, we're having company tonight," Mother said.

The air in the room was crisp. Flowery curtains swayed in front of the open window overlooking the street. When a car passed by, its headlights swam across the ceiling; the sheets of light floated away as the car disappeared down the street. My eyes wandered around the room, taking in the vanity table, the small music box powder jar, the old Singer sewing machine Mother operated by pumping her foot, her fingers guiding waves of flowered cloth under the needle. I picked up Mother's porcelain figurines to test their weight, to see what memories might be hidden inside. I doused my father's Bien-être on my wrist and neck, the underside of my arms, rubbing in my father's musky scent like a salve.

Papa's face tightened. His frown meant *I don't want to see anyone.* He was sweaty.

"But it's Maman's birthday," I said, surprised at my own impertinence.

Outside, mothers shrieked out front doors, brakes squealed, people and their afternoons unfolded. The November sun beat against the window, bounced off my mother's vanity mirror. The blinding white heat stiffened by centimeters, alive, breathing. Shadows fell across the carpet, elongating. I tried to tell a joke to make Papa happy. "Tim Tim," I started, leaning over his shoulder. Knock-knock.

"Quiet!" he yelled, his body a live wire.

He was supposed to say, "Bwa sèch." My mother turned and glared. I wanted to break out of the room, out of the hot, hostile air that filled its every corner. Instead, I floated with Papa's angry words so that I would not drown with them, in them.

Guests arrived. When Matant kissed me, she left lipstick on my cheeks. She measured my every inch because it helped her feel the flow of time and she shook her head, incredulous, her mouth a crescent moon, perfect in its downward curve.

The sound of laughter mingled with the clink of silverware on plates. On the radio, Toto Bissainthe sang to Papa Damballah, the vodou god. Drinks sat away from elbows. Papa became animated, and he was quite the talker. The heat of Christ-Roi focused on him, his face enameled with sweat that dribbled down the bridge of his nose. The gangs of mosquitoes flew up as he mopped the drops of perspiration from his face with a handkerchief embroidered with his initials.

No rat-tat-tat tonight. But I watched Papa, afraid he would suddenly grow horns or a barbed tail. His eyes would turn blood red and while flames shot out of his mouth, smoke would twirl out of his ears and nostrils.

"Dance with me," Papa said.

My father swooped and grabbed my shoulders and I laughed as we spun. One foot hit the table with a dull sudden thump and my mother said, "Goule!" but I could only see her sometimes in the green blur of the kitchen. Nou vire, vire, vire. We turned, and turned, and turned.

"Goule, you're making her dizzy," Mother said.

When Papa stopped, he was grinning. He pulled me into a tight hug and my face fit into his neck like a puzzle piece. Then I was free. My stomach rolled and lurched and I grinned at my father who laughed at me. I was the happiest and most loved girl there ever could be.

The grown-ups talked about politics. They sat in a circle on the balcony and drank colorful drinks, and their cigarettes glowed like fireflies under the tall plants. Papa didn't smoke, but he hunched over a bottle of beer, handsome when he was not yelling. A pretty nice guy, although he still sounded a little mad when he laughed—a loud, hyukking laugh that signaled the madness could flare up unexpectedly, no matter how tranquil he appeared.

My father dominated the conversation to babble about Papa Doc and his dictatorship, about a crazy sharpshooter for Duvalier who would put a cigarette on top of his own son's head to practice his shots.

"Those macoutes were crazy," Guy said, "and, above all, Luckner Cambrone."[8] He leaned back and crossed his arms. If you looked close enough, you could see Guy's stubble—thick, like black ants.

"Prosper Avril's government is a mess,"[9] a tall, lumbering man with a dark mustache put in. He had wide shoulders and oily hair, and a tiny scar beneath one eye. "Duvalier was a dictator, but things were better with him in the National Palace."[10] He put his elbows on the table and stretched the fingers of his hands.

"A dictator is what we need," Guy said, twirling the dregs of his Barbancourt rum.

I wiped the sweat out of my eyes with my wrist. Droplets trickled down my back, under my shirt and pants.

Felicie had been cooking since the afternoon, and the fragrance of frying akra and kibi, garlic and other spices, the guests milling around, laughing and talking, made it like Christmas. Sœur brought out American records to replace Toto Bissainthe. I walked around to show the tooth I'd lost—yellow and ugly. Pitted and scarred and smooth. With a jagged head and a fang of a root.

"Too much sugar," Matant said, mouth opened wide so we could see her white teeth; I glimpsed the small red bulb wobbling in the dark vault beneath her palate. She looked at me seriously. "No more candy for you, mademoiselle. You don't want to find yourself toothless—a dan rachòt."

Mother and Matant reminisced about their childhood. I wanted to slip into my mother's adolescent skin as I imagined her striding down the streets of old Port-au-Prince on her way to Lycée des Jeunes Filles, streets of long narrow Gingerbread houses built so close together you could feel the slap of your neighbors' heels on your own floorboards. I could see it all: She swung bare legs under her uniform as she passed beneath the almond trees, in the flickers

8   Luckner Cambronne, nicknamed the "Vampire of the Caribbean," was François "Papa Doc" Duvalier's second in command and head of his fearsome Tonton Macoutes. He reportedly led a campaign of state terrorism against all opposition, having opponents threatened, attacked, murdered and "disappeared." He dressed in mirrored sunglasses, and dirt clung to his fading army fatigues. A cigarette often dangled from his mouth.

9   Lt. Gen. Prosper Avril was eventually forced to resign in 1990, after 18 months of controversial rule marred by human-rights violations, corruption, and widespread public distrust. According to the *Los Angeles Times*, he went into exile after a dramatic "heart-to-heart appeal by the U.S. ambassador that he leave quickly to forestall further bloodshed." Avril and his family boarded a U.S. Air Force C-141 jet for a 2-hour flight to Homestead Air Force Base, near Miami. The President later became a writer and published *The Black Book of Insecurity* in 2001.

10   Things were not better under Duvalier. People were tired of the dictatorship. In 1986, only weeks before the flight of Baby Doc, a popular band practicing for Carnival in St. Marc dared to parade with a coffin stuffed with effigies of Baby Doc and his wife Michele.

of light and shadow. The streets shimmered and steamed in the heat. On the sidewalk: an accordion in its lively river of song, the music revealing Heaven to her senses.

In Heaven, everyone has his own sky. Everyone knows what shapes the clouds make.

Here, the sky is always the color of chaos.

The lights went off for yet another power cut, and the velvet darkness surrounded us. An earthly, natural hush fell about the house. The music had stopped, replaced by the gentle swish of the zanmann trees in the wind in the garden. The bright light had vanished to be replaced by a dim, somewhat restful blackness. I helped Mother rummage around the kitchen drawer, fumbling for candles. "Must be here somewhere," she said.

The candle burned with a dark yellow flame, and as the darkness dissipated a little, I could make out the lines of the kitchen chairs, harsh edges rounded and softened in the light. Mother gently placed the candle in the nearby bottle. Wax slid from its tip, sealing its new home. Papa rested his chin on his hands, and the light caught the line of his cheekbones.

"Careful with the candles," Papa said. "We don't want the house to burn down."

The candle created yellow-eyed spirits and they danced amongst us with the timid breeze. Matant slapped her palms against her bare calves, and then brushed off the dead mosquito.

"You're always waiting for something terrible to happen," Mother said to Papa. "You have a special talent for that."

"If you say so."

His tone had changed. I held my breath.

The political discussions resumed. People talked about politics and politicians all the time—at the breakfast table, in the car, over lunch, as they reclined in heavy chairs and sipped rum from etched glasses—the talks often animated, sometimes hushed and raw, always familiar, in a language heavy, dark, and rich. Sometimes nothing else seemed to exist in the country but politics. Nothing else seemed to matter. I was sure even in heaven and hell—in between the praising or the gnashing of teeth—Haitians were talking about politics.

"Weren't you one of Baby Doc's informants?" someone asked Papa.

I froze as images of the man burning on Rue Christ-Roi flooded my mind. Didn't that stranger know what *they* did to Baby Doc's spies? The adults were staring at my father. Not a word passed their lips. No sound broke the sudden stillness but the play of a balmy breeze that carried the distant barking of a dog and the whistle of a pedestrian. There were also the incessant clicking of mosquitoes and the guttural chanting of a frog in the garden. Papa's jaw was set. A night bird twittered, and Mother took my hand in hers. I focused on the garden, with its luxuriant flowers, and the sweet-scented gardenia and honeysuckle.

Silence.

My father was not a spy. Papa despised spies.

My mother giggled nervously and everybody relaxed. I was able to breathe. Papa was not getting angry.

Yet.

After the guests left, the house smelled like aftermath.

I must have said the wrong thing. Papa's belt came down across the small of my back. I screamed for him to stop, which enraged my father more. His eyes popped out, and I sensed that I was not the one he wanted to beat—but the nets of some inner demon unraveling inside of him. My heart raced. I could hear the blood in my ears.

Darkness surrounded us. I dropped to the floor and rolled up into a ball.

Then someone broke into a strange peal of laughter. It was Sœur, and her expression had become hideous. "Look at me, Papa," she said.

My father stopped to look at her.

There she stood, on the balcony's railing, arms at her sides, heels together, chest in, her hair, dark and soft, swept back in a smooth roll. Her slender body moved with a mixture of grace and geometrical precision. She lifted her foot and moved it about eighteen inches to the side, then put it back down on the railing. My hands clenched and blood pounded in my ears. Sœur stooped a bit to be sure she had both feet where she wanted them. She straightened up, more or less, and faced forward.

First, surprise—then a mind scrambling to absorb a new and possibly life-threatening situation.

"Sœur, don't," I said.

Or maybe it was my mother.

Or Papa.

It was sixteen feet to the dirt and root-laced ground below.

Sœur landed with a deep thud.

My heart jackhammered against my rib cage. My body reverberated with every pulse beat like a struck gong.

My mother leaned over the railing. "Sœur, are you okay?"

A chill settled inside me, a slight marrow-deep tremor. I scrambled towards Mother and got pulled backwards when Papa grabbed for me. My shoulder knocked into the iron chair on the way. My brown sandal flew off and Mother grabbed it, yelling, "Her sandal!"

He shoved Mother and she shoved him back. Something hurt in my chest. Papa grabbed Mother's arms, and she couldn't move and wouldn't stop trying and started to cry. I wondered if Sœur was dead. No. I heard a rustle down there.

Papa finally let Mother go and locked himself in their room. Just what Sœur wanted.

Mother and I rushed downstairs.

The skin on one of Sœur's legs was broken; the flesh torn in places. I could see the inner layers of white and pink and more white. Large blood blisters rose over her body.

Sœur was in such a state of shock she wasn't even crying.

Blood. So much blood.

Mother grabbed my sister and hurried back upstairs with Sœur against her chest.

So much blood.

The sky was a perfect black and the ruling planets had turned against us. My vision blurred. I could not see where sky reached out and touched the land.

"I love you, I love you," Mother said.

"I'm okay," Sœur said. "Hush."

That's when Sœur gave her the *look*. I'd seen it before— a raging contempt; like she wished our mother out of her life. She hated the way Mother's brown eyes got scared when Papa yelled. She hated her for staying with Papa.

She hated both of them. She told me once that she dreamed of other parents.

What she didn't understand about Mother was that she'd lived a sheltered life in Mahotière, the village of her youth, where days were sunny and mild, the skies a cheerful, eggshell blue, where the river shivered its bright rubble, and sisters lured each other out into the sunshine. I imagined Mahotière, the two-hour hike up a steep, rocky mountain trail among the happy fuchsia of bougainvillea; the acacias that crossed their limbs along the roads; the walls of jasmine, their dark branches covered with white corollas; the lady-of-night vines opening their blue bells in the evening. My mother's childhood village: Heaven.

Mother had been raised to believe that family brought love and salvation. She'd grown up unprepared to face a man like Papa, who wished to punch her, his arm uncoiled in a long-looped Y, the fist as quickly drawn as a crossbar in a T, a man who'd turned her into the sort of woman who went on silent retreats, a woman who could go for weeks in her own mind.

Sœur hid in our room with Mother. I took refuge in my secret hiding place, a closet that smelled of musky old shoes, candy-covered chocolate mints and old varnished wood. A purple raincoat hung on a dusty rail above my head. I ignored the blazed dryness of my throat.

Later, distant blasts of gunshots woke me up. Rat-tat-tat.

Someone had tucked me in the warmth of my own bed, and I was soaked in sweat. I made my way through the house quietly, so as not to alert anyone.

I heard whispers in the living room. The impulse of fear still burned my palms.

My parents sat in the dark, Mother on the sofa, Papa on the tiled floor, his head in his hands. "Where did I go wrong?" he asked.

I was frightened and his tears burned in my eyes. My parents looked smaller, foreshortened. I believed until this moment that boys and grown men were not supposed to cry. But here was Papa, with my mother's hand on his shoulder, crying.

He was tired of the mood swings.

Outside, in the night, where the birds lay huddled, slow-hearted, against one another, the trees were dark and shapeless, and someone beat on a drum, bringing disquiet. Little girls, they're afraid of everything. They don't yet know that the shadows trailing behind them are also a part of who they are.

five

Papa continued to have static rages, anger that shook him for days, until his body could stand it no longer and he collapsed into bed, listening on the radio to chansons of love and despair. Papa's discarded socks seemed angry, fisted and stiff with dried sweat. But in sleep, his forehead was smooth, his limbs still. My parents slept in an embrace, and I saw the curve on one's arm under the other's translucent neck. Looked at that warm flesh. Looked at the trust in those limp limbs. Their dreams, I imagined, grazed each other as they shuffled through the dark. I ran my hands through Papa's hair, which was soft and dark and slipped easily through my fingers. I whispered his name—Goule—a round thing that forced the tip of my tongue to the back of my teeth before releasing wide, like a mouth parted in prayer. Soon he'd be awake, and off to work. And I would long for him, my noisy, careless father, his heavy step, his deep voice filling up the rooms, his laugh. A laugh I wished could linger—a steady vibration against the drums inside my ears. His face looked cuter then, less angled, his jaw less strong, less square. His face became soft as sunrise, his forehead a perfect fit beneath his hairline, smooth and taut. His eyes were a pretty dark. He could be both brusque and tender, my father, in ways I had to get used to every day.

On the balcony, he meditated, serious and dignified, wearing sandals with interlocking straps of light and dark leather. He leaned on the balustrade, watched the street and the man who walked with a limp and the buses that pushed and pulled at their brakes and turned on corners, watched the lines of laundry strung between gray walls stained by azaleas, watched me ride the neighbor's bicycle. As he worried about darting cars and bumps in the sidewalk, the late evening sun settled upon his face, the dust particles floating in the sweltering air. Dogs barked blocks away, their owners or neighbors shouting at them to stop. Through a haze of streets and distances, there was the cry of a child being spanked. A woman walked down the sidewalk in her high heels and crossed the street, the muscles in her calves pumping with each step. She kissed her lover's neck, and he seemed puzzled, like a scolded child, maybe pondering what it meant to fall in love, what it meant to be alive. Like everyone else in the city, he had seen dead eyes, glazed and dry, cried, buried them, stumbled through days of loss. A cop ended his shift, furtive as a burglar.

Papa helped me with complicated homework, when the numbers in the math book wouldn't hold still—numbers like swarming gnats that buzzed about my head. As I completed the assignments, the world had an ethereal stillness, a colorful tranquility. With a knife, he broke a melon, revealing its pink center, its myriad of seeds. He reached for a pink carving, brought it to his mouth, and sank his teeth into it. Pink juice ran out, gathering and quivering on his chin. Or he peeled an orange, losing himself in the color and segments and sparkle of the pulp. When I returned from my games of oslè or colin-maillard, he offered a piece of fruit—feeding a kind of love; if you do it right, it won't be clear who's filling whom.

When he dropped me off at school, mornings looked like this: streaks of amber crowning the hilled horizon, coloring the gray of lingering night. I could tell he wanted to have some morning wisdom, something grandiose and fatherly, a statement to make my day, my week, my life, easier. In the afternoons, we went for car rides around Port-au-Prince, windows down, dashboard peeling in sunlight, seatbelts frayed like catfish whiskers. Sometimes we remained quiet, listening to the thread of the tires run along the asphalt, how they collected pebbles and dropped them back. He'd clasp my hand, Papa; squeeze it, feeling the warmth inside, the pulsing heat of blood.

Sometimes he took me to the mountains, turned up the music in the car, until it was a giant bass roar and I couldn't hear anything else, not even my own mind. The sky was blue and the mountains were green and sheep grazed in the fields. The cherries were dark and shining on the trellis. We climbed higher and higher, the road twisting and turning and cars flying by in a manner both dangerous and natural at the same time. On our way back to lavil, the engine growled, the tires yelped, and he pressed the gas, opening the clutch, counter-steering. The speed made me numb, unable to concentrate on the past or the future. As the sun receded, tree shades turned into deepening shadows. At home, the dog greeted him with his tail in full swing. Twinkle of electrical light from the furthest suburbs scaled the nearest slopes of the mountains. And I was happy for this moment—my father breathing the same air I breathed, our hearts beating to the same rhythm.

***

Mornings, he closed the blinds, blocking the sun. Mother opened the same blinds, inviting light. And so it went: open, close. Inside the house I was always searching, hiding, sneaking around, trying to understand what was wrong with them, the adults. My parents didn't touch each other like two people in love. Neither did they talk that way. They interacted like brother and sister most of the time, and I'd grown to like the fragmented way only two people with a shared history can talk. People who also like rituals—the togetherness in the brushing of teeth, the crawling beneath the sheets, the listening to the gentle night noises of insects discussing the moon. Often they just sat together on the balcony, content with each other's presence, listening to the croak of cicadas, the held breath of the sky. Fireflies wobbled beneath the silhouette of tree branches. A mocking bird, perched on a neighbor's roof, tweeted its many tongues.

They listened to bird songs, their minds drifting and comfortable with each other's silence. Dogs yapped. Buses stopped. Locusts clicked. The voices of neighbors enclosed their house. There was fellowship over bowls of akasan or labouyi. Camaraderie amidst the honeysuckles that unfolded, turned sweet inside, waiting to be plucked, pulled and sucked dry. The moon was full. No walls restrained the air, the darkness, and words were abandoned for other understanding. They loved each other in this silence. It was the most mysterious of loves, I understand now, years into the future. What they shared, I've come to believe, was a sense of peculiarity, a scaly oddness, a deep solitude—even in a room full of people. When they met, they must have thought, *you are just as scared of life as I am,* the realization tingling through their scalps, down their arms and legs. All this time they thought they were alone at the bottom of the fear they kept falling into, but it was not true.

The skies filled with kites of all colors, shapes, and sizes, and the people of Christ-Roi gathered on rooftops and balconies to watch them. No sound on the balcony but the steadiness of breathing. My parents drew themselves, committed their souls, no longer thinking of how, just this morning, they'd been quarreling—their fights now faint and unimportant. Forgotten the slammed doors sending jolts that traveled through my gums, down my spine, bruised the pressed flesh of my knees together. When night came, they were dazed by the full moon, its half-smile anointing their reconciliation. A quiet candle outdid itself in a red glass vase. Despite their disagreements, they had an unshakable belief in their collective future. Sometimes Mother closed her eyes. He took her hand and squeezed it. Both their hands shook, and I knew what it meant: *We are going to make it through this.* They shared something complicated but real.

I could tell Papa liked these moments, the domestication of them. The cat nestled between their limbs, stretched into their warmth or curled against her thigh, his hip. In these moments, the constriction of their insides relaxed to make room for laughter. Sometimes they shared memories—visiting Le Cap together, bare-backing a dogged, spikey-pine donkey, clip-clopping across the mountains, clenching one another, smelling the dirt. Sunshine and birdsongs and green—for miles. And Papa's laugh, of course—it began in his chest and tumbled out and across his frame like waves lapping at the shore of a beach. Everywhere he went, my father charmed to death those he encountered, with his beauty and poetry, his travel stories and charisma, charmed their children, charmed their parents, charmed their neighbors, charmed their maids and yardmen, charmed the birds down from the trees. Papa charmed Mother. He complimented her on her dahlias, orange with red flecks at dawn yet redder with a tint of yellow by dusk. He once rescued a fallen chick, toted its small breast, downy head, broken wing, cradling it in the hollow of his palm. Music made him swoon; he bowed to the jangle of tambourine, bent to the bass player's beat. He listened to the sax and trumpet made malleable by Billie Holiday's limbering voice.

On the balcony, they also talked about the news—about the violence in some distant country. Over there, they were cutting off men's heads. Women were being killed too. Restless students were massacred in Lubumbashi. In our *provinces*, dense forests were reduced to charcoal for cooking fires. As for Port-au-Prince, the city reeked of greed and turmoil and death. The neighbor's daughter, Irma, had been killed, her strange death printed up and lurid in the papers: Irma and that boy who picked her up. He shot her, then killed himself. Papa and Mother spent hours in such conversations, their voices mingling and becoming one, rising, dipping to find the other's pitch. And I hid under the window, listening. I enjoyed how they never talked about what was next, about the fights to come, about who they were together. I worried about them, what would happen to them. In the distance, green mountains draped in white cloud held up the sky.

I checked my father's face often—read for paranoia or rage, studied the shape of his brows and lips, and if I saw an explosion coming, I retreated and looked for my mother's company. Sometimes Mother and I switched places, and I became the storyteller. My stories were not the subtle kind—for the streets were hot with violence.[11]

Port-au-Prince—centuries of conflict, a perpetual struggle for power and vengeance. And still—the sidewalks were jammed with people scurrying along, strolling together, giggling in couples, or chattering in groups. No one seemed particularly fazed by a body under a blue tarp. Another casualty of life.

But that man had been somebody's loved one, and I imagined this somebody—a father, a mother, a third cousin, a fiancée—roaring with grief. Something beyond rationality, an expression of pain deep and primal.

The man had been shot. They'd covered his body with a blue plastic tarp, but I could see his sneakers soaked in red. No police car, no TV crew when Mother's car drove by. Death—abrupt and uncalled for. Pointless. It occurred when everyone else was drinking Fanta, when the shoeshine men rang their bells, when one was simply looking out the window of a white Mazda. Now this man was either singing with choirs of angels or sitting in the eternal workshop that was hell.

I kept a list of random deaths in my weathered Hello Kitty diary. As we drove by, I scribbled down the name of that man—not his real name because I didn't know it. I called him "the man under the blue tarp." In the front yard of the house behind him, laundry lines sagged like shortened smiles. Hopscotch squares were newly painted, but there was no pitter-patter of feet landing on rhymes.

---

11 After Lt. Gen. Prosper Avril was forced into exile, hungry crowds estimated in the thousands looted food warehouses around the capital, and the mob trashed the homes and offices of some of Avril's chief supporters. *Los Angeles Times* reported assassination squads roaming Port-au-Prince to kill pro-democracy leaders, and at least twenty people, including a police major, killed by gunfire. In one incident, uniformed men reportedly mowed down five pedestrians in a drive-by massacre, then raced away with the bodies. Bonfires blocked streets throughout Port-au-Prince. Police used tear gas to repel would-be invaders at a pro-Duvalier radio station, and a bodyguard fired a machine gun to drive a torch-bearing crowd from the home of a former Duvalier official.

six

In 1990, my family moved to Thomassin, southeast of Port au Prince. When the radio relayed fractured news of rebellions, the town of Thomassin, cradled by sharp mountains, held its peace. Presidents moved in and out of the Palais National.[12] A coup was attempted. A priest was elected. In Thomassin, on the earthy paths snaking around the cornfields and orange trees, I ran my hands over the pomegranates' pinkish, shiny hides, their tiny crowns. I reveled in the cracking noise when I bent open the cut seam to expose the ruby seeds clustered together in luxurious profusion. Sometimes the calm worried me, as it seemed unnatural and not in keeping with the news coming through on the radio, the report of the military's rising and the new president's response.

Then it was 1991,[13] and I was ten.

---

12 In March 1990, Ertha Pascal Trouillot, the youngest and only female member of the Supreme Court, was the third woman to become a head of government in the Western Hemisphere. She was a widow in her forties, a nonpartisan democrat and well-published author described by most as both brilliant and patient. A scattering of gunshots and what sounded like grenade explosions followed her inauguration speech at the Palais National. The country's first democratic elections finally took place on Dec. 16, 1990. Father Jean-Bertrand Aristide won 67.5 percent of the popular vote. Jean-Bertrand Aristide, a leftist Roman Catholic priest, was elected president in Haiti's first free and peaceful elections. He was well-known throughout the country for his support of the poor and opposition to Baby Doc's regime. In 1991, Roger Lafontant, former leader of the Tontons Macoutes and former Minister of dictator Jean-Claude Duvalier, attempted a coup against Father Aristide. The coup failed.

13 Jean-Bertrand Aristide's reformist policies alienated the wealthy elite. Aristide had been in office for less than eight months when Generals Raoul Cedras and Philippe Biamby led a violent military coup against him. The coup, according to *NewsHour*, was backed by dissident army officials and partly funded by wealthy Haitian business leaders. After the coup d'état, there was a very well-known song by a popular band from Bel-Air. "I lost one of my shoes. Who can help me get my pair back?" Pè is "pair" and is also "father," and the song is about Father Aristide.

Aristide, the president-priest, was leaving.

The night of his exile, political prisoners were killed in prison—one bullet in each head. Skulls hacked from machete blows, bowels ripped away by blades. I imagined survivors in their cells, huddled and still. On the battery-operated TV, women wailed in loud bursts. In Nazon and Christ-Roi, rifle shots spattered the darkness as the night held its breath in fear. Many were wounded or dead in Lalue.

"The trick when you're under attack," Sœur said, "is to pretend you're dead."

She taught me how to make myself faint. As I leaned over and hyperventilated, she gripped me from behind and held tight across my diaphragm. When I came to, my head was spinning.

The next time Papa got mad, we both pretended to be dead.

I was twelve when Papa got the arsenal. Not just the old rifle he bought from Monsieur Polémond who lived around the corner. I counted two combat knives, two revolvers, a semi-automatic, an assault rifle, two hunting rifles, and a few grenades—round and green, like in the movies.

There was a reasonable rationale for the guns: President Aristide, who had replaced Interim President Ertha Pascal-Trouillot, was in exile in Washington, D.C., and he'd left behind a country in disarray. Citizens needed protection.[14]

Before the coup, before the embargo, I believed Aristide was not any man. He was a priest, after all, and things would be different with him in the Palais National. It was his *calling* to help people, to counsel them and show them the way. He'd get the bad guys to understand that they were not demons, that they should stop hurting each other. Exactly who the bad guys were, I was too young to understand. For me, politics was something cloudy, events jumbled and conflated, time collapsed. My Aristide fantasy: No more rat-tat-tat at night, no more missing school in the morning because cars burned downtown. Our new president was a man of God who would help the whole country

14 After the coup, Brig. Gen. Raoul Cedras did not make himself president. He created the fiction that Aristide was removed constitutionally and, in accordance with the constitution, Supreme Court justice Joseph Nérette replaced Aristide as president at the head of a civilian government that ruled Haiti until the U.S. intervened militarily in 1994. Although Cedras was obviously running things behind the scenes, the international media could not call it a military governmenment (not without being a bit slapdash). The ones that cared usually called it "the military-backed de facto government" or something like that. According to *NewsHour*, the brutal regime used civilian attachés or paramilitaries to support a campaign of intimidation and repression. Several thousand Haitians were killed, prompting the international community to levy trade, oil and arms embargoes on Haiti. Between 1991 and 1994, tens of thousands of Haitians fled the country, seeking refuge in the United States. The vast majority of "boat people" were returned to Haiti.

be good. Change had come. I imagined Aristide in one of the private rooms of the Palais National, where maybe there were Gothic-inspired splendor and paintings of St Ambrose and St Augustine. He wore a zucchetto—no, a miter—and he absolved the repenting mob. The people liked him and trusted him; highly vulnerable and distressed, they treasured the attention and words of comfort he gave them.

Then I heard his infamous words. On my Barbie radio-cassette, I listened to his speech about pè lebrun—death inflicted by placing a tire around a person's neck, dousing his or her body with gasoline, and setting it afire. "Oh, the pleasant aroma," the president said in a sing-songy voice.

Some say that revolution demands violence and death in the name of the future, which for Haiti was bright under the shining sun of the priest's progressive ruling. Others believe that, like many before him, he got caught in the machinations of lust for power. Whatever the case, he was gone and the people were hungry—hungrier than before, because hope was gone too, sucked out of them during the years of dictatorship. The news reported cases of looting by empty-bellied average Joes and home invasions by "sans foi ni loi" (ruthless) thugs.

The home invasion scenario—according to the grapevine—went something like this:

In the middle of the night (one o'clock seemed to be the time of predilection), the children were awoken by violent bangs on the front door. Ouvri pòt la, a menacing voice yelled. Open the door.

The children ran to their parents' bedroom; the adults were already awake by then, the father with a stunned look on his face, the mother crying. The police were called, but the story always went this way: There was drunken laughter at the station, the phone call interrupting a domino game or an orgy. Yeah, we're coming, the policeman offered.

The family believed that the iron bars on the windows and the doors, the multiple bolts and heavy chains would protect them from the zenglendos, but the truth was, the thugs were professional thugs, and they brought friends with them. A dozen men with machetes and guns and rifles—former macoutes, angry chimères[15] (thugs), cocained police officers, whatever. The door proved a feeble resistance. The men got in.

---

15 The origin of the word "chimè" (or "chimère") is disputed. Some look back to a Creole expression, "m nan chimè," meaning "I'm angry," while others link it to the French chimère— an illusion or fanciful idea. In any case, the consensus is that the "chimè" are people who use violence to create destruction and confusion. "Chimè" shouldn't be used as a synonym for "gang member" because gangs in Haiti constitute a complex phenomenon.

The family was often kept alive—because death would be way too merciful after the nightmare.

When many of these stories turned out accurate, Papa got the guns and shot a few rounds at bedtime, so the thugs would know "we've got them guns" and stay away from our property. As members of the educated middle class, we were targets. Papa was a law teacher and Mother a clearing officer at the Banque Nationale. We lived in a comfortable home and owned three decent cars. It didn't matter that Papa worked six days a week and spent the evenings grading papers and preparing lesson plans. It didn't matter that Mother had taken out an outrageous mortgage at her bank and that the house's construction required years and years of privation. We had food on the table while others died of malnutrition and dysentery.

From the green leaves in Thomassin, mockingbirds called. I waved at the dirty children who shouted "tifi wouj" at me, small children and big children with distended stomachs, running through roads that did not have names. I was confronted by cold stare after cold stare. All those eyes looking, they watched me, an outsider, a tifi wouj, unwelcome because my lighter skin didn't allow me to blend in. A mistrust was palpable and terrible in the bitter air, its icy passion carried on the wind.

Whether we accepted it or not, we were the enemy. We were targets.

At night, the neighborhood cracked with sounds. Gunshots. Screams and more rat-tat-tat, the sound of people running, horns and sirens. Then it all faded in the distance. I was awake for a long time, staring at the shapes and shadows cast by the streetlamps on the ceiling, at the roving lights of the passing cars running up the wall one way and then down the other. My bed was not an oasis of softness and warmth, because the stillness in the house didn't feel right. The room felt hot, and I wished for an open door, a window letting in the cool night air.

At twelve, I was no longer a kid, but the shadow of one—childlikeness just out of my grasp, and yet the future fuzzy and dull in front of me. In the kitchen, a sorrowful Jesus watched me from a cross high up on the wall.

In addition to buying the guns, Papa made structural changes to the house. The cement fence grew three feet taller and was crowned with barbwire. The iron gate was also topped with spikes and could only be opened from the inside. A small opening enabled visitors to identify themselves; the tight space wouldn't allow an attacker to aim his gun properly. Felix, our garçon de cour, could duck down or run away if zenglendos showed up.

On Saturdays, the arsenal was on the kitchen table. My father cleaned the guns with a dirty rag under the amazed stares of Felicie and Felix. Papa wanted "the help" to know we were armed and to spread the news in the neighborhood. Because our nanny and houseboy were supposedly part of "those people" who wanted to steal from us.

Felicie had been in our service since before I was born, and Felix had joined the two-people team about five years before. We could trust them somewhat. *Somewhat.* The paranoid mistrust against their social class had reached fantastical dimensions in Haiti. Every stare they exchanged seemed—even to me—like a signal, as in, "The home invasion will start any minute now. I'll go open the gate and let in the zenglendos."

Papa forced square after square of wadding through the barrel of his rifle until the cotton emerged clean, gleaming with oil. He was an unstable man in an unstable country. He was in a permanent rage, yelling, hitting, crashing his fist against furniture, his eyes mean, his lips rippled by the stormy waves inside. I'd lost my papa in some dark hole, and I could no longer reach him. As I watched him break one of his guns, slip a bullet into the barrel, take aim, and fire in the air one night to scare away potential attackers, I prayed to be protected from *him* who slept with a loaded gun by his pillow.

The deep wrinkles in Felicie's face looked artistically carved. I wanted to run my fingernail through one of her skin's trails, feel how far down those grooves went. She was doing the dishes, scrubbing until her back ached and her hands were blistered. She was washing the duller knives in Mother's collection—the butter knives, those strangely shaped cheese knives, and the paring knives used for slicing avocados, mincing basil for pesto, or cutting potatoes. There were some bad knifes in there, cheap ones from downtown. The handles came off; the blades rusted and snapped in half.

Mother sewed at her machine while Sœur practiced scales on the piano. Our dog Pipo had broken his chain again and abandoned the doghouse outside. He watched Papa, lying half-curled, his head resting on his front paws, beautiful with his thumping tail and inaccessible universe. Papa leaned toward him, petted his head, and Pipo wanted to taste something behind my father's calf; the dog's tongue tickled.

Felicie rinsed off the chef knife, paring knife, boning knife, bread knife, carving knife, and truing steel. The kitchen clock ticked faintly, like it was stuffed in a sleeping bag. I looked at Felicie's hands, her hard-working hands that knew too well the soiled corners of a toilet and the dull grating of a washboard. Their calluses were shiny, hard, and round.

Papa's face was stern, crumpled with the strain of age. His thick brows were knitted close together—as if he was remembering something, his cheeks darker than the rest of his face. I stared at that man who could, both literally and metaphorically, go headlong and furiously down one road, and then turn suddenly and quite as madly dash the opposite way—in a matter of minutes. His head was thrown back now; eyes shut, he breathed heavily through his stuffed-up nose. His face dissolved in sweat. It glowed a shiny film.

Felicie had moved on to the Ginsu knife, which cut through tin cans, nails and radiator hoses in the TV commercials. If this knife were ever to cut through someone, there would be muscle contractions and nerve damage. More pain with every throb or movement that caused the sharp blade to cut deeper. Then: the onset of shock. Numbing. The heartbeat reached the ears but the pain died down and everything slowed down. Blood loss made the head swim. The combination of the shock and blood loss might render unconsciousness.

I'd read it in a book.

Felicie wiped her hands in the damp folds of her apron. Now I looked at my father's hands, not nervous, but always moving, stirring sugar into the black coffee, rubbing water rings off his fork, smoothing the napkin's edge between his fingers. Hands broad, sweaty and cold, hands that tried but somehow didn't succeed in smashing Mother's jaw and breaking her ribs.

He spilled some coffee on the table, and the rivulets looked like blood.

As he drove me to school, Papa's fingers played over the steering wheel; he moved the Jeep gently, taking turns with such ease I could barely feel the road rushing under us. The wind whipped my face. The hills of Thomassin rose and fell outside the car windows like the deep swells of an emerald ocean. Scores of billboards lined the main roads with the same photograph of ousted President Aristide, his hands outstretched like a messiah. As we came down Kenscoff Road, which was narrow and winding, a series of steep and pitching curves, the air thickened by degrees. By the time we reached Pétion-Ville, we'd forgotten the tonic of Thomassin, its cool, comforting, mossy silence. On the pavements, money-changers wore Aristide t-shirts in a show of support and waited to take foreign currency in exchange for wads of Haitian gourdes. They sprung out into our path, grinning madly, waving the money.

I barely recognized some of the old houses on John Brown Avenue. The looters had come during the night and taken everything, even the window frames. The houses looked haunted, occupied by some disturbed spirits, the empty windows like drunken, hollow eyes. They gave me the shivers. Sometimes, unexpectedly, people ran and children were trampled in the stampedes, left to die. More often than not, cars burned, their windows shattered by the rocks thrown at them, the remaining glass bloodied during the impact.

On the car radio a lulling voice implored Virgin Mary to intercede for us in purgatory. A sign on a tree read, "Repent. Jesus is coming." The wide streets crossed one another at right angles. The stone and brick houses with their bright walls were close to the sidewalks; business buildings and large frame structures contained the government offices. While we were in traffic, a bum stood by the car, pulled out his penis, and peed on the door. Papa honked angrily.

In front of Sainte Rose de Lima, I kissed my father good-bye.

The all-girl school drew its student body from the middle and upper classes, most kids driven to school by their parents, others by private chauffeurs. A girl in the class ahead of me was the daughter of the French ambassador. We wore white blouses under navy blue jumpers. The nuns, who could be stern and fearsome, but also humorous and warm, paraded in stiff white collars and veils, and I wondered if the sisters had hair under there, or if they were bald.

Papa didn't just drop me off and drive away. He made sure I got in safely, waiting until I bought the habitual gummy rats from Emmanuel, an old, skeletal man with a straw hat. Emmanuel sold homemade doughnuts too, and different kinds of candy that shone under the cool, morning sunrays.

Something else shined on his rack on that day.

Something new.

A pocket knife, the blade smooth.

Something welled beneath the surface and threatened to consume me. I wanted to yell, but I couldn't, because I wouldn't allow myself to become my father. And the knife seemed important, more a key than a weapon—a key to this wildness inside.

I needed this knife.

I could imagine stabbing or slashing, the knife between me and the threat—whatever its face. I could save myself with it, cut my way out.

"I want the knife," I told Emmanuel.

Papa was in the car, still watching me, but I was too far for him to see what I was buying. I had to get the knife *now*.

The man hesitated. There was something different about me he wasn't sure of, something secret. I was electrified, vibrating with tension.

"How much?" I pressed on.

My father honked and raised his hands in exasperation—what was taking so long? I handed crisp bills to Emmanuel. He wrapped the jagged pocket-knife in a paper bag, like he would the gummy rats.

As I put it in the pocket of my school uniform, some kind of force emanated from the heavy metal. Now, I was in control. My world could be in order and I didn't have to be bossed around. I was the master of my destiny—independent, separate from and unreliant upon anyone else. Safe and warm inside. All I had to do in case of danger was pull out the knife and death would swallow the zenglendo—flimsy and slick.

I waved one last time at Papa before I entered the school. I wished he could see I was not the same girl he'd dropped off minutes before. I was a new me—vengeful, cautious, ready to strike. The rage inside was still boiling, but I could do something about it. I was reborn—more dangerous, ready to get in the face of peril and spit. Excitement rose from the back of my neck, an exquisite sensation pulsating throughout my body, turning on the nerve endings in every millimeter of flesh. In my pocket, I pressed the sharp blade hard against my thumb—just enough pressure to feel what was almost pain.

Seven

In her long navy blue habit, Sister Claudette rushed the children to the chapel for morning prayer. In her class, years ago, I'd learned phonics by going to the blackboard and framing the sounds with my fingers. We used an abacus to prove our arithmetic skills. We memorized spelling words like *gentillesse*, *dévotion*, and *enfer*, along with the catechism of the Catholic Church.

I smiled, but Sister Claudette didn't smile back. She knew I'd passed my share of afternoons in the principal's dark, curtained office, reciting Catechism. She knew I was prone to scabbed knees and shirt stains. Could she feel it in the air? I was a new girl with a knife. She tweaked her habit, smoothed her skirt, and gazed around the room with twinkling eyes. I liked Sister Claudette— her wry humor, her quick laugh, the way she paused before she answered our questions, as if she really thought about things and cared about our opinions.

In the chapel, the curtains muted the sparkling morning sun, but beams streamed through the gaps, illuminating the church in restful half-light. Sister Claudette spoke slowly as though mouthing prayer to some considerate, familiar God. We recited the Seven Joyful Mysteries, the Seven Sorrowful Mysteries, the Nicene Creed, and so on. When I spoke in the small chapel, there was an eerie echo and my voice flattened, otherworldly. It was hard to think an archangel wasn't hovering against the frescoes, though more likely pigeons rested there. I imagined Saint Michael's wings the cloudiest white, softly downed without quills or striation, large and strong enough to carry me away in huge, breathy beats.

I sat toward the back, and my friend Estelle joined me. When Estelle walked, the folds of her legs and arms behaved independently from the rest of her body, quivering for several moments after she stopped moving. A roll of fat at the back of her neck curled over her white collar. Whenever she told a good joke, I could feel the stretch of my own enormous, uncontrollable grin. I tried not to laugh, contorting my face with the strain. In the end, I gave up, wiping my shining eyes and shaking my head helplessly. When we met Sister Claudette's scowled face, we quieted down.

When the Canadian priest sprinkled l'eau bénite on the altar and over us, I tipped my head up toward the spray, the holy water catching my face, my white blouse—a cool, weightless refreshment. Father Olivier led us into prayer. The words tumbled out of his mouth. He told us we would probably burn infinitely in hell but if we prayed hard and often enough, there was a chance we wouldn't. During the song, *Alleluia, le Seigneur vient vers moi*, I thought about the knife in my pocket. How it could slit a throat, Ninja style.

I imagined its blade inscribed with vodou vèvè, and the metal glimmering with a thousand colors. In my imagination, it was made from a morsel of the moon that had plunged to the island of Hispaniola when Caonabo, the Amerindian, still ruled the Cibao. Maybe Nicolas Ovando plucked it from the fingers of Caonabo's wife, Queen Anacaona, before she was hanged in Santo Domingo. When Ovando was recalled to Spain in 1509 by King Ferdinand, the blade remained on the island—worshipped and feared for its power. It might have been lost to history for hundreds of years before it emerged again, taken by Papa Doc from one of his witch advisors. This knife cut through women's wombs, cut out the eyes of opponents to the regime. Until, finally, after its journey of eons, it somehow came to me.

A merciless knife.

My knife.

My fingerprints already covered it. Later I would trace my initials on it with liquid paper, in slightly messy cursive. I didn't often mark my name on things. I was not of the type that liked to scream out *mine mine mine*. But the knife wanted me to belong to it. I wanted to belong to the knife.

A silver chain, with a tiny Virgin at the end of it, dangled around Estelle's neck.

"Juliet Fanon," Estelle said in a whisper. "She was killed yesterday."

My breath came out shallow and quick. I waited for grief or sadness to match the news but all that came to me was a sense of something gone from the world, although I did know Juliet quite well. We all did, because she was involved in Student Activities. I remembered her face was puffy, like she'd been crying for years. She was a Daughter of the Virgin, and carried a rosary in her pocket. She once said I was removed from my own life. She said I was missing some important ingredient to make me whole, real, full, complete.

Estelle told me more of the gruesome story. When she said a crew of bòs had been working on the family's unfinished house, I imagined the masons— the rocks, blocks, and sand wheel-barrowed onto the worksite, the mortar mixing, the buckets of fresh wet mortar handled by a chain of sweaty workers, the foundation walls filled with ranblè. The men poured cement, their shovels working quickly in the gray mud, scraping the edges, mixing them into the gooey center. The wheelbarrows squeaked as they were pushed closer to the wall the masons built. The men's brown arms corded from the strain, the muscles on their backs bulged down to their waists.

Juliet was alone. At lunchtime, the workers left, except for the one who cut her with a knife.

I felt sick, but I was also fascinated with the specificity of the imagery of Estelle's descriptions. I was *there*. The attacker had been a fat, dull kid, with a startled expression and clammy hands. There was something off-putting about him, even in adulthood, so that most people distrusted him on instinct.

I thought, Juliet is dead because she let her guard down. For one minute, one *second*, she forgot we were not safe.

I never allowed myself to forget.

The blade in my pocket had ripped through the paper bag and felt hot against my palm. *Thou shall not kill.*

I would kill if I had to.

I would kill if I felt threatened.

I would kill if it came to it. Better them than me. Something wild was growing inside me. A rage that tried to understand and that tried to survive in a messed-up world, a world in which the twelve-year-old I was didn't just worry about the color of her lipstick, but about gang attacks and sex crimes.

I wanted to believe it something nobler than the beast that inhabited my father. I wanted to believe the rage inside of me grew out of self-defense, out of desire to protect not only myself but those I cared about. That it was not an untamed fury that stroke against everyone—including those I'd vowed to love. But maybe I was no different than my father. And any moment could change me—what made me, what was born in me lay still for now, but I might explode one day. I might become my father, rageful with misery. Any moment might turn me. And there was nothing anyone could do about it.

I couldn't go back to being what I'd been before, pretending to be untouched by the ugly things in this world. I was no longer a child—a timoun piti. I was not yet a woman, and I couldn't see the point of being in between.

I recognized myself less each day. I gave a lot of thought to Father Olivier's warning against hell. I could not be a good girl, moral and virtuous like the Virgin Mary. I prayed to the Heavenly Father, my Papa Bondye.

"I'm going to confession," I told Mother.

It had been more than a month since I'd acquired the knife. She didn't know about its pointed stainless steel buttcap. Its thick blade, nearly five inches long and partially serrated. Its overmolded handle, which prevented hand blisters and provided a secure and comfortable grip.

My head was cradled in her lap as she braided my hair—glossy, black, and thick—in the muted silence of dawn. I giggled when her fingers brushed against my neck.

"Kenbe tèt ou. Keep your head straight," Mother said, her breath as sweet as a mandarin.

I endured the tugs and the hair pulled too tight.

"It will loosen up over the day," she told me.

It never did. My eyes were left squinting.

Mother took a break between braids to drink coffee. She drank it with a passion, as if, when she awoke to the chill of the house, the horror of the Port-au-Prince streets not yet underway, comforted by the smell of dark coffee, she could keep the illusion that she was safe. She brewed volumes of Café Rébo, drank it down to deter the inner chill from overwhelming her. Beneath everything I knew in our house in Thomassin—the smell of Foltène in Mother's hair, of Jean Naté on her skin, the kitchen, smells pouring from different corners—was the scent of Mother's coffee, the anchor of the real world.

"Okay, we're done." Mother put down the comb.

In the kitchen with beige marbled floors and wooden linoleum counters, the table was sticky with coffee. I knew the map of the cabinets, knew where to find the pistachios, the grapefruit jelly, the box of cheese balls. For the past weeks, before each spoonful of cornmeal porridge, I'd silently prayed to God so He would give me the strength to cut the enemy's throat if it came to that. Now I prayed to Him to make me a good girl.

Maybe I should fast. Yes, before confession, that was probably the right thing to do. Lent was too far—I needed to be good *now*. The anger boiling inside me had become an emergency—I couldn't wait for high mass and low mass and vespers. What if I got out of control today? Why couldn't we do the Stations of the Cross everyday, for the sake of my soul? I suddenly wouldn't have minded kneeling on the cold marble floor in the kitchen for long hours, eyes closed, hands raised to Heaven. We needed more services too. At mass, the high school kids, beautiful in their dark blue jumpers and crisp white blouses, sang with a far-off stare, their voices lifting up to the chapel's dome, and Mother stood with the other awed parents, holding her sheet music, searching for her part.

Students lined up in front of the outbuilding that served as confessional at Sainte Rose de Lima; we stood under a canopy of trees blooming madly with pink pom-poms. At first, I led the line of repenting students, but because I was chewing chiclet, Sister Claudette pointed toward the end of the line. "Come back when you're ready."

Her voice reverberated. I wondered if Sister Claudette knew I'd stolen the grapes, raw and sour, from the vineyard last week. I wondered how she would react to the knife in my pocket. I imagined the rotisseries of Hell where I would roast hundreds of years for these sins and the ones I wanted to commit. Without the knife, my only weapon would be my bitterness. I took a deep breath; the fist in my chest tightened. I hoped Father Olivier would be able to help me without my having to tell him about the knife.

During confession, Sister Claudette waited outside the confessional, counting the minutes of our sins. "Are you sure you told him everything?" she asked outside. Hair like a tiny bird's nest grew on the bridge of her nose.

While the students awaited their turn to enter the confessional, she explained Juliet's death by talking about God's will—divine reasoning, she said, is beyond the grasp of human understanding.

When it was my turn to give my confession, I got ready to talk to this masculine higher power that was God. The walls and windows of the confessional were covered in condensation; the corners of the plastered ceiling darkened with rot. In a small mirror, my face looked disfigured, melting down the glass. Father Olivier, a plump, well-fed little man from Quebec, with full cheeks and a flushed face, sat calm, spine straight. His eyes, heavily hooded, made him look tired—or bored. He sucked his white teeth in contemplation, as if they were sweets.

There was no booth—no darkly hidden, vulpine shadow within. The priest sat on a wooden chair, and I used the kneeler in front of him, bowing my head.

I was tempted to tell Father Olivier about the knife in my pocket. Not out of intimidation, but because maybe he could save me from the anger inside. I was not going to Heaven with a sparse faith. Unless I changed my ways, when I beat my chest three times and said *Notre Père*, probably no one would be listening, not even Father Olivier, who still did his magic trick of pulling forgiveness out of thin air. I pushed my face into a look of penitence.

Father Olivier put a hand on my bowed head. As the cool skin of his palm cupped the back of my skull, I told him about the blade; how I often admired its jagged silhouette with all of its implication. How I sometimes imagined an attack: the knife entered a collarbone, and a downward stroke punctured the lung, the heart of a zenglendo.

"Am I going to Hell, Father?"

No answer.

When I lifted my head, Father Olivier was dozing, elbow on his knee, palm cupping his cheek, mouth slightly opened. Sweat had soaked into his face.

The knife I carried in my pocket clattered down, and the priest awoke with a start, his lashes batting back the mid-day light, now grown intense, suffusing the narrow space of the confessional. I bent down to get the knife before Father Olivier could notice it.

"Papa Bondye loves you," Father Olivier said, unperturbed.

He sent me back outside where Sister Claudette waited, eyes wide and unblinking. Here was this lover of God. I could not be like her. In this I found a dark and fitting comfort in place of absolution. Pigeons flew over my head, their cooing like firecrackers. Around the chapel, bush burst with song, cries, and strange animals glimpsed through the trees.

Days after confession, Sister Claudette called me in her office. She held her hands curled around each other as if in the midst of prayer. "Is Jesus a part of your life?" she asked. "Just curious." A morning of frowning had creased deep lines between her eyebrows.

She didn't wait for an answer. "There's a promise for all people—no matter who, what, when, where, or why."

I wrinkled my nose but kept silent, my throat crowded with hot words. My eyes burned. My pulse twitched. On the wall, Virgin Mary stood demurely in swimming-pool-blue robes, with palms folded and large imploring eyes. Jesus, on the other hand, had a burning stare.

Sister Claudette heaved a deep, irritated sigh. "God says, 'If you draw near to me, I will draw near to you.'"

The sun streamed in through the stained-glass windows. The airy light caught the dust motes, and they lit up like stars. Outside the windows, the grasshoppers and crickets sang and whined. Drying grass crackled.

In my pocket—the knife.

"You're double-minded," Sister Claudette said. "Uncertain, half-hearted. Interested in following Jesus but not willing to change your heart." I listened to her voice, the sweet cadence of it. "We call it wanting it both ways. The good and the bad together."

The cicadas streamed into the deepening blue of the morning sky, the day hot and bright.

Sister Claudette tut-tutted, even though I hadn't said anything. "Sin deceives, and the Father of Sin and of all lies is Satan. He is the one who lies and says you can have it both ways. What happens when someone tries to walk down the middle of the road in Port-au-Prince?" A sliver of hard flesh bobbed up and down at her throat. Her voice rose, cracked on the last syllable, her face growing flushed in the excitement. "What happens?"

I let out an uncomfortable laugh. "They get hit."

"Exactly. Walking down the middle of the road will get you run over. You have to go to the right or the left. Not the middle. You need to walk with God on the right side. He sees the good in you but also recognizes your confusion because the heart of man forever dwells on evil, unless it is changed. Only a surrender to Him can cause that change to take place."

I laughed again, until I cried, then couldn't stop crying. I cried on Sister Claudette's lap, without telling her why. She peered into my face, her forehead arched in concern. Then she prayed. I hoped God was listening hard, because even I couldn't hear the mumbled words. I pleaded with God for strength and purity of thought. My knees ached.

I must have faith. With the light turned off, I could barely discern the stars out my window that night, but I knew they were there and I looked into darkness until sleep took me and stars no longer mattered.

Sister Claudette persuaded me to become a Daughter of the Virgin, and put me in charge of the morning prayer. To God, I wrote poems that made students weep, that occasionally rose the hairs on the back of my own neck. Each week, I read the Scripture and based my prayer on Saint Matthew's writings, and each prayer in its meticulous stages of shaping came closer and closer to an utter sincerity. I read the Bible, cover to cover, searching for some nameless thing. I read about early martyrs and medieval saints, about virginal women—stabbed, tortured, or locked away because of their devotion to Christ.

In my pocket—still the knife.

I thought about its sharpness, how easily it would slide through an enemy's flesh. My grip tightened on it. I imagined how it gleamed.

The Daughters of the Virgin met on the playground—la cour de récréation— on Fridays. We dropped to our knees to start with a prayer. Immacula, our group leader, read the Apostles' Creed. "Je crois en Dieu Tout-Puissant, créateur du ciel et de la terre." We answered, "I believe in the Holy Ghost, the holy Catholic church, the communion of saints, the forgiveness of sins, the resurrection of the body and the life everlasting."

Immacula was an older student from high school. Short and thin, with hollowed-out cheeks and sunken eyes, she looked haunted, as if she no longer belonged to this world. She led again with the Lord's Prayer, "Notre Père qui est aux Cieux, que Ton nom soit sanctifié." Her hands clasped the rosary beads. In the sky, a low line of blue-gray clouds moved slowly, creating a dying, shifting light.

"The Glorious Mysteries," Immacula said. "The first Glorious Mystery, The Resurrection." Voice chanted: "Hail Mary, full of grace, the Lord is with Thee. Vous êtes bénie entre toutes les femmes." We answered, "Holy Mary, Mother of God, priez pour nous, pauvres pécheurs, maintenant et à l'heure de notre mort. Amen." An unreasoned anger caught along the base of my neck like needles.

I thought about the screams I heard at night, beyond the neighbors' rusted-out fence with the gaping hole the rats climbed through—a woman screaming for the beating to stop, the husband raging.

"Do you hear that?" I'd asked Sœur one night.

"I don't hear anything," she lied as I stood at the window, trying to pierce the night, to see the small hills like lumps in the street and the houses rain-soaked. Lightning created sporadic, brilliant veins of fire.

The nights the woman screamed, Sœur pretended to sleep so hard she was like something that didn't breathe, her body stone-like under the blankets. I believed she refused to acknowledge these screams because they reminded her of our own screams, whenever Papa's mood swung.

I'd tried to see the man my mother met, more than twenty years ago, and pictured another version of my father—younger, compelling, sweet. Sometimes, however, it was impossible to imagine him in any way, in any state, other than this one: yelling. What had my parents seen in each other? I wanted to know that. I wanted to come to that place where I might understand the two of them. Otherwise, I would never find anchor.

Estelle (whom I'd persuaded to join the prayer group as well) got the rosary from Immacula. It was time for the second Glorious Mystery, The Ascension, and I hoped Estelle wouldn't hand me the beads; I didn't feel like leading. When I turned away, Estelle gave the beads to Caroline who started, "The third Glorious Mystery, The Descent of the Holy Ghost Upon the Apostles."

The nights the woman screamed, I waggled around and adjusted my pillow, threw it on the floor, stared at the ceiling, then reached for the pillow again, put it back under my head because nothing helped; it didn't matter. I couldn't stop hearing the screams. If the neighbor lady had a knife… I imagined the blade sinking into the husband's lung. The body—limp.

In the morning, Mother brewed coffee. She had the radio on, and she commented about the news, how terrible things were, and didn't I think things in Haiti were terrible? She pretended the couple next door hadn't filled the evenings with screams and curses, and for some reason her betrayal and confusion sickened me.

When my turn came, Immacula noticed my reluctance, so I went ahead, "The fourth Glorious Mystery, The Assumption of Mary Into Heaven." The wind rippled through the flamboyant and ylang-ylang trees; it moved through them like waves. After I slipped the beads to Lola, my eyes kept closing. I tried not to doze. When we said the rosary, Immacula watched, so my mouth had to make sounds.

During the day, the neighbor lady was quiet—she endured whatever there was to endure.

Until night came.

Not all her screams were alike, and after a while, I could distinguish one from another. Some were sustained, operatic; others were quick, sharp stabs. A few were in-betweens—mid-screams. Then the night became a coat of blank silence.

Only the Litany and the Hail Holy Queen were left. When I closed my eyes, Mother's face came to me clearly, her eyes haunted with loneliness, and I wondered whether I would be like Mother, kind-hearted and generous, or like my father, full of temper. I often scared Mother with how savage and feral I could be, some fury boiling inside me. I was too young for the rage I'd learned from Papa. I was too young to carry a knife.

We continued our prayer. My voice rose through my throat, and I was surprised at how smooth it sounded. "Que ton règne vienne."

The woman cried in the night. *I wonder why she doesn't use a knife to kill the bastard.*

Things screamed inside.

eight

Papa decided the house must be haunted and called for help.

The Freemasons came first because Papa was an initiate.

The two gentlemen looked solemn—Mr. Napoleon with his black suit and tie and shiny leather shoes, and Mr. Gerard with his tan suit and brown shoes.

"What seems to be the problem?" Mr. Napoleon asked.

Mother had been working in her new garden when they arrived, so she was still in a sleeveless shirt and the top was unbuttoned, revealing the mysterious line of her cleavage. Strands of her hair had escaped her bandana; her shoes were soiled and muddy. When the late afternoon light had ebbed from the room, she turned on the gas lamp. The pale light spread in gloomy shivers, illuminated the dining room table with its oilcloth cover, the mahogany shelves on which pans and kettles stood, and the cracks on the walls. I sat in a dark corner and ate quenêpes. Elbow on the table, I watched the flame dance at the end of the wick in the gas lamp. I also listened to the sudden, furious, whipping rain outside. The unexpected rain pummeled the pine trees in the garden, the cement walls, the tilted roof. The wind blew in through the edges of the windows and moved the flowery curtains.

Papa, also in suit and tie, told Mr. Napoleon about the cats. "I think they were demons. There were at least thirty of them under our window last night and their meow sounded more like a cry from hell."

Overwhelmed by the wailing of neighbors, I hadn't heard cats cry in the night. I suspected there were no cats—only a woman being beaten to death. But Papa insisted the cats danced in the night full of dark shadows, and Mother offered a reluctant explanation.

"Our home is built on an old crossroad, where offerings used to be made to the spirits. The gods were not happy to see this crossroad disappear, and they're letting us know."

Mother had gotten this piece of information from Madame Sorèl, the lady who sold her goat milk and pork. The cats must have shaken up Mother, for she usually didn't talk about such sornettes—nonsense. Weren't educated people to dismiss superstition?

"I shot one of the cats," Papa said. "We saw it fall on the lawn, but found no sign of it this morning."

"The maid witnessed the whole thing too," Mother said.

I understood that Papa wanted these guys to perform some kind of exorcism and drive the spirit cats away. My father wasn't a church-going man, but he was considered a good, honest, decent citizen, and was respected in the community. If he said he'd seen strange cat-ty creatures, that was the truth.

Mr. Napoleon stroke a match, lit the incense he'd brought with him and rang a chime. A gray smoke curled up, and the fumes filled the room with an acrid, intoxicating odor. I held my breath because I didn't want to take in the heavy smell of incense that stung my throat and mouth, already dry from drinking Mother's Manischewitz wine.

Sister Claudette said once the Devil couldn't stand the aroma of incense.

In the swirling smoke, the faces of the men were eerie as their sonorous voices intoned strange words in a strange language. I wondered about what went on inside a Masonic lodge room. I didn't remember Papa going to the lodge; I didn't remember it ever being a topic of discussion at the dinner table. I thought again about Sister Claudette who despised secret societies. When she sent our report cards home for Papa to sign, Sœur used lemon juice to make the three shameful dots—the three pillars of Masonry—disappear next to his signature.

I followed Mr. Napoleon and Mr. Gerard around as they called upon the spirits and energies living in the house, inviting those who would be harmonious with the new household to remain, and asking those who might be happier somewhere else to leave. I waited eagerly—and in vain—for a possession to take place, for devilish laughs or cries.

During the prayer, our hands swapped sweat, slipped, reclutched. I couldn't concentrate on what the men said because Felicie and the gardener, gathered at the kitchen door, peered in at us with disguised amusement. Felicie giggled behind her hand. Maybe she thought my father had lost his mind.

The sun slipped its last light through the close branches of the pine trees. After the gentlemen left, Mother allowed Felicie to pour some special oil around the house as well. Apparently, we could use all the help available. We were Catholics and believed in an almighty God, but books on white and black magic, Rosicrucian teachings, Freemasonry and vodou practices stacked Papa's shelves: in the midst of political and spiritual turmoil, we didn't know what god to turn to. Who knew what evil awaited? Before he'd been ousted, our Catholic-priest president had encouraged the mob to take "justice" into their own hands, to steal from the "bourgeois," to destroy businesses, and burn down fancy houses. Was it true? For me, politics remained undefined, with its obscure allegiances, incessant speculations and accusations.

Love, too, your enemies. Pray for those who persecute you.

I loved being a Catholic. I loved our small church in Thomassin, dark and cool, the soft, blue tinge and the irregular shapes of the glass tiles that depicted Orthodox saints and scenes of the Bible. I loved the chanting of Veni Creator Spiritu, the statues of the saints and the Virgin Mary, with her smooth, serene face and her outstretched arms. Father Martin, one of the priests in Thomassin, wore an elaborate robe with gold and silver threads that sparkled in the candlelight, and the smell of incense weaved into his clothes. On Sundays, head bowed and hands together in front of my face, I made my way toward the altar; I genuflected, knelt, tilted my head back and stuck out my tongue to receive the Body of Christ. I was awed by the centuries of rituals.

Later that week, Mother invited Father Martin to our home for a house blessing. The neighbors joined in the celebration with a joumou soup, bright yellow-orange with an opulence of meat and Caribbean vegetables. The festive occasion included Haitian Cola Champagne, cake, a spiced concoction of kleren,[16] and thick, spiked kremas.[17] Papa even bought Barbancourt rum, Prestige beer, as well as imported cocktails for his fellow law professors. People came in fancy cars—people who smelled good, tanned women with cleavage, men with cigarettes.

The mosquito coils kept most of the mosquitoes away, but once in a while, a hand slapped a calf or waved around a neck to swish away the fierce, hungry buzzing. It was dark around us, but the patio rested in a small pool of light, our faces half-light and half-dark, mottled with shadow.

Father Martin had an open smile on a small mouth, puffy red cheeks, and bright blue eyes. His presence connected me to something profound, a source of stability, permanence, and transcendence. I was allowed to smile, but not

---

16 Domestic rum.

17 A drink made with condensed milk.

to interrupt the adults who talked about the coup and the embargo,[18] about political prisoners starving to death in the prison in Port-au-Prince.

I sat alone in the kitchen. After a visit from the Freemasons, some vodou oil, and a Catholic baptism, all the gods should have been satisfied. I could still smell Mr. Napoleon's incense, and I knew there should be no more cat dances under the window.

And yet I still heard the cries of our neighbor lady.

After the guests left, Sœur came clomping in the scraggly grass across the yard, making the bugs fly, yelling about a book I'd borrowed without permission. She who never yelled. She who was small and skinny with dark, soft eyes that avidly studied the world around her. A quiet child who concentrated intensely, her fingers trapped in some science book. Sometimes she read detective novels, sometimes the lacquered glamour ads in magazines. She read books thoroughly from beginning to end, as she did not believe in skimming or jumping pages. She studied hard in the evening, doing her homework, one subject after another, one, two, three hours straight.

In photos of Sœur and me, I was always much bigger: heavier, thicker boned, thoughtless in the way I claimed space. She was skinny but filled the air with her presence.

"The book," Sœur said. "Give it back."

This was not my sister. This was a girl possessed. This place was changing her too. Her lips were puffy and raw like she'd been licking and biting them. Her voice was a screech I did not recognize. The Sœur I remembered had a melodious cadence.

As she screamed, an inordinate rage and breath-catching irritation built within me. I tried hard to control it, but my sister, water to my fire, yin to my out-of-control yang, wasn't showing her usual temperance. My own fury came like one hundred horns and one hundred bells. My nerves a chorus of plucked strings, a quiver of quivering. The blood in my fingertips pulsed.

"Shut up," I said, my fingers balling, my hand making fists.

Family was supposed to be a safe zone. The petunias nodded yes, yes to the wind. Brown-winged butterflies mingled and bees scribbled invisibly over hibiscus flowers. The sun shot black spots into my eyes while the wind moaned like a low fire. The knife in my pocket was heavy. My jaws ached as I clenched them to keep from screaming.

I grabbed the glass bottle of Fanta I was drinking and threw it at Sœur.

---

18 The United States and other nations imposed a trade embargo, but it was partly circumvented by smuggling through the Dominican Republic.

She gasped. The bottle hit the wall and broke into tiny pieces.

Look what we do to one another, I thought. The world was dangerous. Something deep in me needed to be tapped, rooted out. I had thrown the bottle at my sister on a day that had seemed plain. So that I could never trust myself, so that every day from then on held in its purposeful or dreamy breaths the possibility of precipitous rage. While Sœur usually remained subdued, I was violent and easily angered, brutal and cruel when I fought.

I tried to suck in air, the heaves from my body terribly loud: frightening. My sister hugged me and I let her, and I held on, her heartbeat against my chest. Its beautiful, crazy boom boom. A drum beating. A cup of sparking fireflies. As I cried, her fingers nestled in the ridges of my spine.

"Can I sleep in your bed?" I asked, even though it was hot. The kind of hot that made sleeping next to another person absurd, the pulling apart of skin moist and elastic.

I looked at Sœur in the stutters and twitches of sleep, her arms in disarray like fish confused by waves. Her body flinched, and it clicked, and it dreamed. The flickering of eyelids, like moths that slowed their flight before landing. In the bed, we pressed together, each filled with the other's emptiness, the other's trop-plein. Gray light fell through the windows, a disorienting, dusty light. I looked at the flitting shadows on the wall, listened to a car outside, its roar, its violent, rattling bass that summoned all of Thomassin. My head pillowed by a length of arm, I listened to Sœur's breathing—each inhale's up-strum.

The first time I actually used the knife, I wore gym shorts, a white polo shirt and a cap that read "Keep it cool"—for basketball practice after school, on campus. It was 1994. I was in the eighth grade. It was one of those humid afternoons, when Sister Claudette's red and pink roses filled the air with their musky smell; the chapel's bells rang four o'clock, and the cowbells clanged on mini-ice cream trucks on John Brown Avenue.

Farah, our basketball coach, was a slender girl from the high school, with short, brown hair that framed her face and hazel eyes. Students said some girls in high school smoked cigarettes, drank alcohol, and made out behind the lockers after school. Practicing my lay-ups, I wondered about these rumors, about Farah, picturing girls kissing girls, girls fumbling each other's breasts shaped like lotus buds.

Because Farah said we could beat the team from Sacré-Coeur, I practiced dribbling the ball for hours—I dribbled through my legs with my right hand, then switched to my left hand and dribbled from the back. We were not always defeated, but we did lose more often than not. Farah, however, was positive:

We would win this time. When no one was looking, I practiced exotic shots. I never missed a day of practice, even though there were no showers at school to clean up afterwards, and my skin was slick with sweat until late in the afternoon, when Mother picked me up in her white Mazda that played a jewelry box song when the key was left in the ignition. My mother listened patiently to the long details of my day, to my endless talks about Coach Farah and the adroit dribbles of Estelle, the team captain.

I wanted to win this game, but Estelle didn't really care about basketball, preferring to chat noisily with Lola on the bleachers, where they brought ti carole ice cream and cheese balls. *Something* needed to go right in my damn life. *Something.* Anger boiled inside me—a bodily emotion. It lived in the entrails, a malevolent parasite. My stomach cramped violently, a wave of sickness.

"All right, *all right!*" Estelle moaned when I reminded her about the upcoming game. She shrugged. I thought of quicksand—if I were being dragged under, Estelle would give the same shrug.

On the court she didn't try very hard, missing her shots, laughing instead of focusing on her style. Lola smiled at my exasperation.

"Okay, girls," Farah said after an hour. Her voice trilled in the upper register to indicate emphasis. "See y'all after school for the game tomorrow."

Lola followed Estelle and me to the lockers, where students had scribbled nasty notes about the teachers. When Lola said nonchalantly, "We're gonna lose anyway," I grabbed her by the collar and her head hit one of the lockers. "Why are you on the team?" My eyes pricked with unshed tears but my mouth felt warm and alive.

The knife in my pocket—I wanted to fist it.

Holding Lola like this, I felt less spectral, less insubstantial, less invisible. My body became a tangible thing, shoulders and arms and hands.

Estelle stepped back. She removed some Juicy Fruit gum from her mouth. She said, "Calm down."

Lola waited for me to hit her, a blank look on her face. She had a thick, square face. Her large mouth drooped downward at the corners. Her cheeks glowed like coals. "We always lose," she said.

Maybe I ought to show her how scared she *should* be of me. I could press the blade just hard enough to draw a drop of blood.

The smell of sweat filled my senses. I let go of Lola, my fists still curled. I watched her leave. She kept her head up.

I took out my knife and violently stabbed the wooden locker door. I never knew that kind of meanness in me. Things inside me moved toward something I didn't know, and couldn't come back from.

"Whoa," Estelle said. "Where did you get this?"

The steel knife went nuts, whacking against the wood like gunshots.

Lola didn't show up for the big game the next afternoon, and my only shot hit the rim.

"You scared her," Estelle said. She chewed on another piece of Juicy Fruit gum.

Part of me was glad I hadn't scared Estelle. I hugged her.

"Somebody is feeling better," she said.

We lost after one of our girls scored in the opponent's basket. I caught Coach Farah in tears, in front of the wounded locker door, and her weakness disgusted me.

nine

My father's theatrics took away my sleep. I let myself believe dawn would change everything and stayed up all night to prove it. After all, the Egyptians believed the sun burnt up each evening and rekindled in the morning—a fresh torch for the day.

As the minute-hand of the clock moved, though, the house continued to feel like a trap. Papa sucked the air out of my existence with his chaotic mood changes, suicide threats, and rages. Time became an object, something that burned the tongue and lodged in your throat to choke you.

Night moved its limbs through the land. Outside, frogs throbbed, impossibly loud for such small bodies. In my bedroom, it was dark and the smoke of mosquito coils curled in the air. The mosquitoes still whined, the piercing whirr close to my ear. I looked out the window, toward my neighbor's house. An ancient car, propped up on cinder blocks, rusted in the driveway. Cheso was in his front yard, with three other men, their faces large, their clothes dark. The smell of marijuana swayed towards me along with the hum of the generator throbbing light into the neighbor's house.

The men outside my window put huge trashbags in the back of a beat-up Datsun, and I remembered Papa talking about the drug deals that took place at Cheso's house. The men laughed and smoked cigarettes that dotted the night like fireflies. I knew I shouldn't be watching, but I couldn't help it.

A woman sat on Cheso's porch with a cigarette of her own. Her baby suckled at an exposed breast and the woman looked worried and cross. It wasn't the look mothers have when a new baby has been born. Jimmy just sat there. He was Cheso's oldest son, a skinny, angular boy with a tiny patch of stubble on the tip of his pointed chin. Dogs lay belly flat on the veranda, pooling saliva under dripping tongues.

Then suddenly, something was going on.

"Men lapolis, men lapolis," a man cried. The cops are here.

I hadn't heard the patrol cars, but men in uniforms surrounded the place, brandishing batons and shotguns. Cheso had firearms—I'd seen him polish his arsenal on the porch—but it was too late. He was on the ground, his pudgy arms behind his back in handcuffs. Jimmy and the other men were sprawled next to him.

"Pa tire," the woman begged, standing. "Don't shoot, baby."

She had wide-set eyes. She waved her hand in front of her face as if shooing flies. "No, no, no." And she did a jig. "Don't shoot, baby."

The police didn't pay attention to the woman. The baby yelled when his mother yanked him away from her sagging breast.

The neighborhood mocked the woman. *Don't shoot, baby.* They did the jig to go with it—cruel but funny. No one cared about the crying baby.

Felix, our houseboy, told me about the gossip. He was shirtless in the sunlight as he cleaned my father's car, and he had burnished-oak skin, high and honeyed cheekbones. There was a rhythm in his movements, like a pulse, when he ran the dirty rag over the windows and wheels, as if he had all the time in the world.

"I saw the whole thing," I said.

I was a big shot because I knew the story. "*Don't shoot, baby,*" I said. I imagined the woman's toes, the knuckles tufted with hair.

Felix nodded. He was in charge of the yard, but on Felicie's day off, he made us Aunt Jemima pancakes—large and thin. Papa stood with hands clasped behind his back in the style of a French maître d' while Felix demonstrated the proportions of milk and powder. I watched Felix too. In the kitchen—throwing flat pancakes high up in the air, like on a cooking show. In the vegetable garden—his hands running on the stems and undersides of the tomatoes leaves.

"Go back inside."

It was my father in short pajamas that stopped halfway up his thighs. His upper lip curled in contempt: I was not supposed to chat with moun sa yo, with the help. I felt misplaced, as if haunting my own body, embarrassed, and I needed to justify my presence at Felix's side.

The sky was blue, the air still. I looked at Felix—but not at his eyes. I wondered about his age. Twenty-one? He'd told me once that the doctors had said he would die before reaching his first birthday, because of a deformity in his heart. His younger sister died before he did—she choked on a quenêpe. At her funeral, "Jesus, pitié" exploded into jazzy blues from a saxophone.

When he talked and stumbled into the stories and anecdotes that amused him, Felix's smile spread and squinted his eyes; wrinkles appeared on his smooth face. He was great at telling stories, Felix, and I could listen to him forever—but the barriers that rose between us made us turn our backs to each other.

"Hurry up," my father said again. "Go back inside."

Anger pressed something grave into his face, thin lines into his forehead. As for me, I was a ghost made into temporary flesh by my passion for stories.

And these stories kept coming. Another man was arrested in the neighborhood for drug trafficking. The next day, his mother-in-law Astrid died of an aneurism, surrounded in her garden by rhododendrons nodding in the first breezes.

"I knew Astrid," I told Felix.

Astrid had let me inside her house the week before, shown me the shrine built for the Virgin Mary in the small room under the stairs. We'd sat in the living room, careful not to step on the rug shaped like a flattened tiger with an impressive head sticking out.

She was open, her smile immediate and honest. She talked to me like she would with an adult—her marriage was troubled; her husband was leaving her. Later, she offered me a bouquet of black-eyed Susans and bought a fifty-dollar tube of toothpaste from my Amway magazine.

Astrid's flowers wilted and curled before I remembered to vase them in my bedroom.

"Don't worry about it," Papa said. And he bought me potted flower plants to counteract my loss. Begonias and snapdragons, small but already in bloom, like fuzzy pink tongues.

The begonias did not thrive.

I still brought the snapdragons to my face to inhale the sweetness.

After the flowers, Papa bought me a basketball hoop and for hours the iron craftsman worked on putting up a pole and a wooden rectangle. Papa held me in an awkward embrace as we watched the electric stars fly around the drill. I tolerated the hug, taken by the excitement of having my own basketball hoop. The next day, after Father Martin behind the mesh window told me to say ten Hail Marys for wishing my dad dead, Felix and I leaned against the chicken coop and ate ripe tomatoes from the vine. Felix told me about the years he'd spent in school, about his speech disorder that made the other children pause, then laugh. In first grade, the words rose from his throat like damp, nocturnal creatures in an unforgiving light. After the sixth grade, he didn't return to school.

"Inside," my father told me. Then to Felix: "I need to talk to you."

The next time I saw Felix, he avoided my gaze. When I asked him for a story, he said he had work to do, reminded me that the world was divided into two classes: the people who cleaned and the people who could afford to treat the people who cleaned as if they were commodities.

At dinner, it was just Papa, Mother, and me. Sœur was at the neighbors'. We were a handful of actors playing a normal, functional, happy family on the set. I was steaming inside, furious about Felix. I tried to let go of many things, only to discover their accumulated, sticky insistence.

When Papa went on and on about his students and how exceptional they thought he was, how they felt they could come to him—the model citizen—for advice, I lost it.

"They don't know you," I said. The knife in my pocket emboldened me.

The room went still. From across the table, I caught Papa looking at me, his face the face of a stranger, as if he were trying to figure out who I was, or why I was in his house. Something flashed in his eyes, something fierce and furious that would normally shock me silent and make my stomach coil against my spine. My father dropped his fork loudly onto his plate. I held his gaze—his eyes huge, dilated, fixed intently on me. His lips were a flat line and his eyes hard in his face, burning. He had that mad look about him, that thickened "I'll break your face" demeanor that would frighten anyone.

Mother was perched on the edge of her seat, ready to fly away, hover over the room. She took a breath, let it out, closed her eyes, then opened them.

"What is the matter with you?" Papa asked, biting out the words. His voice was strained, his breathing ragged. The white of his eyes caught and reflected the light. These were the eyes of a man who didn't know I was armed and dangerous.

I swallowed as a lead weight settled in my stomach. But I went on. "We're miserable because of you."

With her eyes, Mother warned me I had already gone too far. I'd challenged the authority of the family head, and defiance would not be tolerated.

"I hate you," I said, my voice unwavering.

But saying these words made me realize how untrue they were. His cheeks sunk in, the way they always did when he was mad. The panic crept up from the base of my skull, making my scalp tingle and tighten. It swelled beneath my breastbone.

I expected my father's chair to slide back, waited for him to lunge at me across the table, to swing his long, powerful arm. I imagined the blow catching me on the cheek just in front of the ear. In my mind, I spun out of my chair, crashed against the fridge. My glass of lemonade tipped over. Dishes broke on the floor. The world darkened and then returned, glittering in tiny specks. A rain of sequins.

But Papa didn't run at me. He didn't kick at me with his foot. Pain didn't explode in my ribs. I didn't have to put my hands up to shield my head.

Papa stayed in his seat, horror on his face. My eyes met his and I did not look down, letting the seconds pass, letting the look on his face settle in my memory, the breath coming out of me ragged. His graying hair jutted straight out on top of his head. I saw a desperation seldom found in his eyes before, and I wanted for him to gather me up in the circle of his arms and carry me to a place of comfort.

"Why don't you shoot me?" he asked.

I sat stunned and silent.

"You know where the guns are," he said. "Get one and put an end to it."

I was surprised to see the tears come up in his eyes, and even more surprised to feel tears in my own. For a moment I remained still, tense and undecided. A fog drifted through my mind; thoughts seemed familiar, but their shapes obscure and distorted. *I can end it.*

"Or use a kitchen knife," Papa said. "Just kill me."

"Stop it," I said.

The hand touching the knife in my pocket shook, and I put the other hand down on my jeans to steady it. Papa's eyes bulged out of his head. The knife felt heavy in my pocket, and I was close to cutting him somewhere. My hand was still shaking. I tried to slow my pulse by taking deep breaths. It didn't work. I imagined the rage burning deep in the pit of my stomach, and each breath ignited the flame brighter. My bones had disintegrated, leaving my legs wobbly and weak. I wanted to jump out of my skin and run.

I wished to reach into Papa, tame the beast inside him.

The house had a heartbreak of its own, pulsing with space, waiting for me to take one stand or another. I could choose to use the knife. Or I could choose to walk away.

I left the kitchen.

I wrapped the knife with old newspaper and threw it in the garbage can in my bedroom. The night was beautiful—full of damp earth and the high calls of nighthawks. I lay back in my bed and allowed my bitterness its exit, with a breath I let out the hate, let it drift from the window and into the dark.

ten

In the homeroom, students slammed their books down and pressed chewed chiclet to the undersides of desks. Chairs squeaked and books rubbled onto the floor, the pages of these books curling with use as though they were burning slowly. The overhead fluorescents buzzed to life, and the room filled with a shaky, friable light. On Wednesdays, before lunch, we took Scripture Class from Sister Claudette, who brushed the wimple back off her shoulder as if it were a fall of long hair. She told us Bible stories. We prayed and held hands and sang Jean-Claude Gianadda songs. We clapped. We hopped up and down. When the bell rang for recess, girls in blue jumpers with white blouses spilled into the halls, yelling across the throngs to each other.

Estelle and I hid behind the bushes near the chapel. I thrust my hand inside my backpack, rummaged around until I pulled out two bottles of red food coloring. Estelle poured some red number 5 on her hand and rubbed the cool liquid on her arms.

On the playground, smooth calves dangled from monkey bars. We joined the other students and Estelle staggered and collapsed on the grass. I watched the grass bend in a long sweep as the wind blew over it. The blades whispered mutinously, each one dangerous, reckless. A group of children surrounded us and two girls shrieked when they saw the "blood" on Estelle's body.

My friend couldn't hold it for long. Laughter erupted from her throat, volcanic, watery. "April fools!" she cried.

Cynthia and Melissa frowned at our dark humor, but Caroline and some others joined the fun by splattering the red liquid on their skin. Lola lay on the ground—*Look, I'm dead*—and she did look dead, motionless, her neck stretched back, her hands and face and hair covered with the thick, drying substance. Her brown eyes were wide, staring ahead in shock and pain.

I played the doctor. "We've done all we can for her," I said in a dramatic voice, "but she lost too much blood." I paused, as if to allow the girls to process this information. "Normally we only allow family members to see the dying patient," I continued, "but since the president-priest had her relatives killed,[19] we'll make an exception."

"I should have been a true friend," Caroline whispered. She sat next to Lola and held the girl's hand. "You've lived a tough life."

Alexandra took over. "May you rest in peace."

We did not hear Sister Claudette approach. "Whose idea was this mess?"

Everybody pointed at me.

"April fools?" I suggested.

Sister Claudette frowned from under her gray and shaggy eyebrows. She dragged me to the classroom by my ear and was about to spank me with a wooden ruler on the palms of the hands when we heard the first shot—and people screaming in the street. Students came running inside the classroom, and I helped Sister Claudette close the thick wooden doors that we chained from the inside. We hid under the desks. The walls muffled the fusillade of shots, the babble of shouts and counter-shouts.

I lay like mush, hardly blinking or breathing.

"Stay down," Sister Claudette said in a calm voice as she lay next to me on the wooden floor. In her presence, I was safe from the blood and gore and stink and whatever destruction was in the town. She was praying. She had lost her veil in the commotion and her white hair, as soft as dawn, brushed against my face.

After the shooting, life went on, like it always did—people were born, people died, people ate, drank, sang in the shower, clipped their nails, wiped their butts, did the everyday things people did when they lived. At school, we still learned poems by heart, which meant to hold them in our minds and recite them. Those of us who couldn't were asked to stay after and practice.

The nuns organized a school fair, a Journée de Couleurs—a blur of colors and smells and sounds. The sky was full with bobbing balloons, which danced around the sunrays poking through the clouds. Under the flamboyant tree, the hot-dog lady covered the sausages with mustard, onion, pickle, tomato catsup, and hot pikliz. Breathing in the greasy goodness of ponmkèt cakes and the sugar rush of cotton candy, students, with their dark blue uniforms and white ribbons, spent their centimes and gourdes on popcorn, peanuts, homemade ti Carole ice cream, hamburgers, and Styrofoam cups of orange

---

19   Some accused President Jean-Bertrand Aristide of fomenting violence to further his political aims.

soda. They bought deep-fried foods, tickets to shows and athletic tournaments, and enjoyed rides and prizes.

Mothers who had volunteered to man tables frowned at students speaking Creole, a language they considered vulgar—the language of the masses. "Mais, qu'est-ce que ça veut dire? Français, s'il vous plaît, Mademoiselle!" They discussed the drought in Plateau Central, where the riverbeds were just dust and cracked earth. The ground was a powder that turned feet and ankles light brown.

In the elementary school yard, they had brought a mare named Madame, rented out by the Equestrian school in Delmas. In history books, I'd seen Toussaint Louverture ride a horse in battle and explorers cross unknown lands on horseback, and on Sundays, I'd watched *My Little Pony* on the American channel. I'd dreamed of riding, although I'd never seen a real horse up close before.

I gently approached the animal, with her long, graceful neck, great solid legs, hooves like buckets, and huge chest. Her skin was black, her tail and mane white, eyes dark and wide, and her coat was bright copper. She had white markings on the face and legs. I watched the girl who sat in the saddle and held the reins. It could be *me* up there. Madame arched her neck proudly, and stepped daintily around mud puddles, as if afraid of soiling her feet.

"Twenty-five gourdes," a man said, squeezing the last sip of orange soda from a straw. Bernard, Madame's trainer, wore a stylish, hard hat—the kind made for riders, tight-fitting pants, boots, and a light vest. "Twenty-five gourdes and we let you ride."

The girl jumped off the horse, a thick braid hanging heavy halfway down her back, and Madame seemed tense. She laid her ears back flat and squinted her eyes. A bit uncertain about getting on, I took the reins, reached up and grasped the saddle's pommel. I wished I had a helmet, along with boots and long pants instead of shorts. My exposed skin would chafe from rubbing but I wanted to get on the horse.

Bernard cupped his hands for me to step into, and as I mounted Madame, I accidentally kicked her in the flank. Startled, the horse leapt forward, nearly unseating me as she ran blindly into the trees. Madame's legs stretched far ahead; I tugged desperately at the reins as she settled into a lumbering gallop toward the chapel.

It was a wild ride—branches ripped past my face, nearly sweeping me off the animal's back—but somehow I held on to the horse as I tried to guide her. I was not big enough or strong enough to force Madame to stop; the entire body seemed synchronized in a forward motion.

It was a lonely experience, the animal's ribs hard against my thighs.

My heart pounded faster than the horse's hooves on the cement; I tried to regulate my breathing, tried to hold this engine underneath me at a steady pace.

Bernard yelled, "Be in control!"

In front of the chapel, the horse stopped with a snort. Madame reared up, trying to turn round first to the right and then to the left, but Bernard waited for her, his face melted into a shriveled scowl. The horse balked and threw her head up, but I hung on, heart in throat, whispering, "Gentle, gentle."

Bernard calmed her down.

I waited a moment, face flushed with heat, sweat streaking across my face, as the whites of my eyes, I imagined, were still bright with adrenaline.

During the ride home from the fair, sitting on the scratchy gray seats of my mother's car, looking down at my dirt-encrusted tennis shoes, I recalled with tremendous clarity the ride on Madame, how I feared I'd be scraped off on a tree and lie winded and wounded on the ground waiting for someone, anyone, to come and rescue me.

Under the animal's labored breathing, the thudding hooves, I'd realized that Bernard had assumed I was capable of riding—just like Mother assumed I was strong enough to deal with the horrors of Port-au-Prince and the drama at home. Not once had she tried to explain to me why so many dead people were recorded on TV, and why my father was so angry. At thirteen, I realized that life in Haiti was a mad ride, and no one bothered getting me a helmet.

Mother wore her michèlbenèt glasses that afternoon—huge dark things with lenses that bulged out like fly eyes. We rode in silence for a while. She drove meticulously, even coming to a full stop at intersections.

"I don't understand," I said.

"What?"

"Why did you marry him?"

Her fingers tightened on the wheel and she jammed on the brakes. "I don't know."

Silence.

A cop behind us leaned angrily on his horn—we'd stopped at a green light. Mother's head jerked around so quickly the bones in her neck popped. She lurched the car forward. Dust blew along the pavement, and heat waves bounced off parked cars with curly bumper stickers.

I wondered about my father. When he gazed into a mirror and into his own eyes, did he fear the proximity of that other face glaring wildly at him through the glass? I watched my mother, who wouldn't swoop and shout and would not attack. What dreams did she keep sheathed sharp and deep in her heart? The way I saw it: She had fought against him and been ruled by him for as long as she remembered. He was the source of all her trouble and all her glory. A failed marriage, I'd heard one of her friends at the bank say once, is the greatest source of sorrow in a life. Divorce is a horrible thing, a mystery, a dark surprise, the worst thing that can happen in a family, except for the death of a child. That's what the friend at the bank had said. And there was a mile gap between what I understood and what I could explain.

Mother seemed to have just woken from some horrible dream. "Wh—?" She was shocked—as if I had a secret I had never divulged to her, an unknown compartment to my life.

The familiar sting of embarrassment rose on my cheeks but I insisted. "Why is he the dad you gave me? You had a great father. When you tell me about your childhood in Mahotière, you're all energy, bouncing around and talking quickly. Why would you be so selfish and marry Papa?"

I stomped my feet on the car rug several times, startling gray dust into the air. My mother did not look at me. The line of cars moved forward and she depressed the brakes. A bare-chested man drilled a jackhammer into the asphalt, his skin pouring sweat. The road choked with foot traffic and vehicles.

Mother turned toward me; she squeezed my hand, and I felt a flash of safety and warmth.

"Your hand is cold," she said, disapproving. But she didn't turn the air off.

I took my hand away. "I don't understand," I said again, looking at her.

Silence.

Was she thinking about her childhood in Mahotière? She talked about her father, Pa Roger, in reverent tones. She loved him, loved the stories he'd told her—about growing up in France with his Mexican mother, and later moving to New Orleans where men and women danced their hips and feet to the drums, while their lips spilled laughter as brittle and shrill as clinking glasses where sugary sweet tafia flowed. She'd told me how her parents met in Port-au-Prince, after Pa Roger arrived in Haiti to become the manager of the Railroad Company. How my grandfather fell in love with the young woman selling movie tickets at Paramount Theaters. How Grandma Clara wore a gray beret on top of a head full of black curls. How her laugh ran clear across the street. How Pa Roger went over to find out her name, tried to speak to her, but Grandma Clara was not interested. She wasn't like other girls who chewed their cuticles and jiggled their legs nervously. She had a strangely straight mouth, a determined jaw.

I was jealous of this uncomplicated love Mother was allowed to feel for her own parents. Her childhood was my phantom limb, the thing once flesh, now gone but living as a restless pricking under my skin.

I pressed my hand against the window, still looking at Mother. She frowned, scolded me—without facing me—for leaving fingerprints on the glass. I wiped them off with a napkin from the blue box on the dashboard. It left a streak, however. I wanted to be mean, but Mother's anxious glances bore down on me, a physical pressure, so I relented. I became ashamed of the questions I'd asked.

People milled about in the streets, lips moving, probably chatting about what they were doing for the coming weekend and the rest of their lives. Others rode their bicycles among the young men in crisp shirts, and the women, curvy and without makeup, wearing flowered dresses in the heat that slowed their bodies. A guitar player performed on the sidewalk outside a coffee shop; two men drank maltas in front of a bookstore.

I wanted to tell Mother I was sorry, but I didn't know how. Embarrassed by my impertinence, I lowered my eyes. Mother took a lock of my hair and wound it around her finger.

"You know," Mother said, her voice strained and her knuckles showing white as she gripped the wheel. "Things are not always black and white." She blinked and then she frowned. "Life is complicated."

A thick fog enveloped Port-au-Prince. No clouds of shimmering butterflies feeding on black-eyed susans; no multi-colored trogons with their feathery underpants, blue-and-white tails, honey-yellow beaks, and gray chests. Giant wet drops ricocheted off the hood and splattered against the windshield.

e!even

How pretty was Port-au-Prince on Saturdays, the streets still askew but drained of the crowds. No masses of people rubbing against each other. Port-au-Prince was not tremulous with busloads of school children. The shoeshine men huddled in front of the bakery, which smelled sweetly of pen rale, French bread, and beef patties behind its closed doors. Hands slapped knees when laughter erupted—volcanic, stretching the cheeks under straw hats. Soon the Epicerie de Lourdes would let the children wander in for bonbon lanmidon cookies and mints shaped like small boulders. Young men scrubbed the pavement with Mistolin, ça fait la joie de mes narines. Someone wakened the drunk, slumped like laundry. In some front yards, clothes hung suspended from the lines.

Behind the wheel of his Jeep, Papa didn't miss a bit of the city's awakening, turning his head this way and then that way. The vendors of fresko slushies were out—grenadine was my favorite, with crushed peanuts on top. Never mind the flies and the mosquitoes. Mikwòb pa touye ayisyen. A girl at my school said the ice came from the morgue down the street. Never mind this girl. Sa je pa wè kè pa tounen. What you don't know doesn't slap you in the face.

"Look," I said. "It's one of those mad men."

Port-au-Prince had a lot of crazies parading in ragged military garb, their faces mud-smeared, more bone than flesh, their eyes bottomless, their hair stiffened with dirt and lice. Women sitting behind their big pots of fasomur fed them because the good word said, "For I was hungry and you gave me something to eat."

When I got out of the car in front of the school, a tall man trotting by knocked my leg with his briefcase and bustled on. A lone taptap idled at the light.

"I don't understand," Papa said, "why you can't be well-behaved. Why do you have to speak your mind and get Saturday detentions with Madame Lemoine? You could be watching cartoons on Télévision Radio-Canada. What is that show you like? The one you enjoy so much you gave up Saturday ballet lessons on account of not missing it. Ah, I remember: *Félix et Ciboulette*."

An old woman sat in front of the school, selling ripe and green bananas, tangerines and mangoes. I wondered where she spent the night. She didn't ask you to buy a fruit, nor did her eyes condemn your wealth.

"*Félix et Ciboulette*? That was years ago," I said, waving good-bye. "I'm too old for kiddie shows, Papa."

I liked Saturday detentions. I liked the Latin déclinaisons Madame Lemoine made us study during the session. An hour into the detention she forgot how badly I'd misbehaved. I sat close to her desk and she told me about her own childhood teachers. About the one with the birthmark across the nose, who'd tied a student's left hand behind her back, forcing the right hand to trace the loops and curves of cursive writing.

"Be good," Papa said, adjusting his eyeglasses in the rearview mirror.

Another father dropped off his child, their complicity evident in the way she spoke to him, animated, the way she hugged him without reserve.

We could not be friends, Papa and I.

Madame Lemoine. Seventy years old. Always carried an umbrella. Kept her nails clean and well-manicured. Her tailor-made clothes smelled of Fab laundry detergent. Her head unbowed, her cheekbones high, she sat behind a desk stacked with Geology quizzes and French dissertations. She'd been teaching Mathematics, Philosophy, and Chemistry for more than thirty years, and had been manning Saturday detentions for that long, too. Students feared her because she was stern.

That was not the Madame Lemoine *I* knew, though—lost in laughter and exciting stories about summer vacations in Les Provinces, cooking recipes from Carrefour and Bwadchèn, and anecdotes about the days of Papa Doc and later Baby Doc. She knew about our history, about the Pompons Blancs and the Pompons Rouges, and the sordid details of the hanging of Queen Anacaona. She told me about Mother's Day in the old days, about the flowery brooches sold in front of the Sacré-Coeur before and after mass, about the customary liqueur rose and ponmkèt pound cake consumed at lunchtime. As she reminisced about her younger years, her hands helped her do the talking. From time to time, she interrupted the flow of words to ask, "How's that déclinaison going?" But she knew she'd spare me from reciting *a-a-a-ae-ae-a/*

ae-ae-a-arum-is-is because she liked an audience and would rather speak about Old Port-au-Prince than thrust me into silence and Latin.

As she told me these stories, I was the center of the universe.

I hadn't fooled her—she knew I chose to be here. On Saturday mornings, I didn't mind leaving my bed full of plotted dreams when the sky sat awake above us, when shoeshine men carried their world in a box slung across their shoulders, ringing their bells. Yes, the first time, I deserved the punishment for calling the English teacher an ignoramus. However, after some quality time with Madame Lemoine, I'd learned to orchestrate my misbehaviors so that I ended up in her detention room. I knew which teachers had a short temper and just how much to speak my mind to get a "Saturday" without La Direction creating a permanent file about me.

The other girl, Valerie, had a permanent file. She sat in the back of the room, away from us, her ears waxy, her shoelaces tucked under the tongues of her shoes. Uninterested. Uninteresting.

I shared some stories with Madame Lemoine too. I didn't tell her about the knife I once owned, but I told her about Jean, my old neighborhood's loony. In Christ-Roi, Jean always looked at his shadow, puzzled, and walked with a stagger, his skin bruised and crusted with dirt. I was visiting the neighbors one day but it was naptime and the house was asleep. Leaning over the railing of my neighbor's balcony, I yelled, "Jean, oh, Jean! Over here!" How crazy could he be? Well, the first rock hit the choublak hibiscus flowers growing in Madame Ville's giant brass pot. The other one Jean threw at me landed on the roof. When Jean left, Madame Ville brought out a belt. I knelt on the cold marble floor and extended my palms. When the punishment ended, I was sent home hot with shame.

From time to time police sirens howled outside, piles of garbage caught fire and smoke hugged the sky.

Madame Lemoine liked me. She liked my prose notebook, the doodles I traced around my poems as if they were memories of her own adolescence. I used to think I was the only one who stayed outside of my dreams, an intruder looking in my own sleep as people acted out scenes in stories, but Madame Lemoine said it was the same for her—she was an outsider in her own dreams. I glimpsed a smile on her face when I thumbed my nose at the other kid and laughed. She told me about the children in the neighborhood, the uncultured teenagers she worried about. The neighborhood of Lalue, she said, sauntered badly forth—rotten pilings, cocaine, quick sex. Some mad kid killed the neighborhood cat with an umbrella. The zenglendos—if they didn't shoot you with a gun, they cut you with a knife. "Those are the real crazies," she said. "Not your harmless hobos. These are criminally insane."

She said once that maybe I loved stories too much.

When Papa picked me up, the sun was still shining. The shoeshine men had set up a table in front of Epicerie de Lourdes and they played dominoes, their faces frowning, but a smile only inches away.

It would have been impossible then to imagine Saturday mornings could come to Port-au-Prince, vacant of Madame Lemoine.

When I heard, years later, about the home invasion and the zenglendos, about the cords that tied her to a chair, about the gag, about the strangulation, my fingers touched reality's face, my own face dirty with tears. The hands of clocks had spun to make me older then. I stood before the smudged bathroom mirror, toothbrush in hand, and I saw myself as I was then—a thirteen-year-old kid with a Latin book sprawled on her desk, displaying the wrong page. And Madame Lemoine still alive, telling the story of Remus and Romulus.

Her words still rise like a dream chorus in my head. I am left with a store of memories—the scent of her herbal rinse, for one—and a wave of longing sweeps through my body. Yet the absent face begins to tatter, fading, going out.

I think of rain clouds rising over the city, the afternoon giving way to cold rain and beaten down grass.

Rest in peace, Madame Lemoine.

twelve

There were several killings in nearby Raboteau,[20] so Papa got more guns and rifles. He taught Mother how to load a rifle magazine, strip and clean, shoot to kill. I watched him strip his guns and clean them; they lay on the bedroom floor in pieces, and the room and his clothes reeked of gun oil afterward. Papa let me press the magazine full of bullets. One night, when zenglendos tried to get into the neighbor's house, Papa put the Uzi on automatic and emptied a magazine in the dark. The sound of the gun cracked the air and hit me above the belly. My father's eyes were bright, hungry, and quick. With no warning, his glare might drop you.

I stayed in my room. When there was no blackout, I turned on the TV and flipped through comedies and dramas and game shows and talk shows and the commercials between them. I watched even the unwatchable—weather conditions reported by Capitaine Météo in a throaty voice. On Télé Haiti, a woman spoke about the trade embargo against Haiti; she said it was a way to punish our military rulers for not reinstating the country's ousted elected leader, Jean-Bertrand Aristide. The public schools would have to close because the average Joe could not afford the increasing price of gasoline and taxi fares.

Private schools, such as Sainte Rose de Lima, opened their doors only three times a week and families decided to carpool. Non-school days were unsupervised, as parents had to make their way to work. On non-school mornings, Mother dropped me off at Estelle's. This arrangement worked fine for me—more than fine, actually, as I was fond of Junior, one of Estelle's friends. I was eager to fall in love and kiss and call some cute boy my boyfriend.

---

20 An infamous massacre happened in Raboteau, a seaside slum about 100 miles north of Port-au-Prince, where several pro-democracy activists were killed. Brig. Gen. Raoul Cedras was accused of having been the intellectual author of the massacre.

Estelle was often home alone, but that piece of information I kept from my mother.

Sometimes one of Estelle's friends picked us up, and we ended up at some guy's house in Delmas, surrounded by high-school-aged boys. If one of them were hitchhiking on the road, even in daylight, you'd lock the car doors. Boys chewing their fingernails and wiping their faces on their shirttails. Boys with their hands on the hips they tilted up, boys with their arms akimbo. Their smallest moves seemed magic to me. And yet I looked for my father in their faces. Sometimes the resemblance was there—dark eyebrows over mean eyes. Those boys would become men: They would yell and hit; they would want their women in aprons; they would want their dinners on the table as soon as they walked through the door. They would want their women quiet, subdued.

But still—imagine lightning in the night, when suddenly the world turns bright and the harsh positions of objects are revealed, before they slip back into darkness. Sometimes, a man, a father, will look at you in a way that makes your heart open like a moonflower. You'll see how afraid he is that you might fracture and break—like dots in a pointillist painting. You'll see how afraid he is that he might be to blame. You'll see a desperation you have seldom found in his eyes before.

And people will not always understand when you'll try to tell them: where's there roughness, there's often tenderness too. Your muscles ache with pangs of longing for this father you know must exist underneath the one who hits because he doesn't know what else to do, the one who moves through the stark murkiness of an overwhelming sadness, the one who's lost God and other relations because they cannot share his secret grief.

It's deeply physical, this longing. You miss that other father so much it feels like a second girl trying to push from your torso, to struggle free from your bones.

In a corner of Estelle's living room, a boy named Vincent taught me how to play chess. We sat on beanbag chairs next to a marble chessboard, with gray squares and shining blacks. But I was distracted by Junior, his limpid eyes, his exquisite smile. His lips were full, like pomegranates, his chin firm. I'd scribbled his name in diaries, on bathroom walls and borrowed books. Junior and Brigitte, Estelle's sister, watched the news instead of the Champ car races on Channel 5, because there was more heated action in Port-au-Prince these days than there could ever be on any race track anywhere in the world. They sat on wooden chairs, backs against macramé pillows, legs stretched, bare feet stacked on the living room table, toe to toe. Estelle and Brigitte's parents were at work, their grandmother at the doctor's, so ice cold Prestige beers and Coke cans disappeared from the fridge, while the people on the screen protested the embargo on Haiti and the high prices of gas. There comes a moment when all that's been denied rises up and leaves you raw and trembling.

"Look at this mess," Vincent said. "Maybe Aristide shouldn't have left Haiti after all."

"I bet the U.S. military will bring the priest back," Junior said.

I'm sure they knew I was faking when I nodded my head and widened my eyes, pretending to understand the drama of Haitian politics. They knew—because they were faking too. Yes, Port-au-Prince smelled like the pursuit of riches; when the wind blew right you could sense confessions of hundreds of crimes. But we were just children. We only knew what the media reported—machetes dripped gore in neighborhoods, people got shot, stabbed, and strangled.

Lola and Estelle whispered outside, on the balcony, under the lush, green rows of vines. They shared stories and nightmares. While I spent hours reading Victor Hugo and writing short stories, Lola and Estelle snuck into nightclubs and smoked cigarettes on forbidden road trips. They smoked pot together and wore black lace under their school uniforms. I was too boring—a girl who kissed and told. Sinned and told. We left a store once with unscanned Twix chocolate bars. I was the one to hike back into Caribbean Market in the pouring rain, plunk my buck down on the counter, and tell. "I don't think I paid for this." I had an innocent look about me too. Wide-eyed and sweet, Junior had told me once.

Lately, however, instead of being the serious girl who watched news coverage about Aristide, the embargo, and la vie chère, I'd been secretly reading racy books and I wanted to be a wild girl—like the American women I read about in magazines: Sharon Stone, Madonna, Shannen Doherty. I wanted to become the kind of girl who wore thick black eyeliner and was audacious enough to know what she wanted and what she was made of. Raw, authentic and radically in love. I wanted to smile bigger and ache deeper. Astrologically, I should have been a Gemini—two separate entities swimming in opposing directions, doomed to battle the other's current in an ever-churning sea. I no longer believed in the rite of confession and no one could force me to reveal anything to a man sitting in the half-light of a confessional room.

The lights flickered and the TV was off. Blackout. In the semi-darkness, Vincent groaned and Junior stretched. Alice, the maid, brought in a kerosene lamp. There was no more gasoline for the Delco generator.

"What now?" Vincent asked.

We were running out of ideas to fight boredom. Two days before, we'd played endless rounds of Clue and Monopoly, and put on swimming suits to make silly dance moves in the rain. In the living room, we slow danced, low danced, and fast danced. We belted out Salt-N- Pepa, crooned to Coolio, and swooned to the New Kids on The Block. *Step by Step!* We played our music loudly, so that the bass thumped on our heartstrings.

"Let's go on the balcony," Brigitte said.

In the warm afternoon, the soft breeze stirred the great trees and the flowering bushes. I wore a summer dress and open-toed sandals. On the balcony, Estelle smoked a Comme Il Faut cigarette. Lola relaxed on the hammock, listening to Buju Banton's Murder She Wrote album on her CD player. Alice got us some snacks, and we piled next to a wooden table, arms twisting to reach for Chico cheese balls, Pringles, the ashtray, "cheese, please," "my lighter," "a beer." The clouds boiled up on the hot summer afternoon and, in the sky, I saw the fantasy images of my dreams—Junior's lips, his furrowed eyebrows. A group of clouds took the shape of a car. I was ready for any road trip he would take me on.

When the lights and the television were on again inside the house, I found myself alone with Junior on the balcony. Aristide was on the air, promising his prompt return to Port-au-Prince. My unsupervised days would soon be over. I would be once again plain ole Jessica.

"Do you want me to kiss you?" Junior asked, his eyes probing.

I pretended these words did not awaken a storm inside of me. "Do you go around kissing girls?"

"If they're pretty," he admitted, unruffled. "Ever been in love?"

I was curled up, my legs wrapped in my arms. "Once," I lied.

In the backyard, Alice worked at her sewing machine, her face wrinkled and damp. Her son sat next to her, leaning against a pillar, guitar in his arms, playing a song from long ago, before the priest, before the chimères and père lebrun, before the embargo.

"I wanna be him," Junior said.

"Who?" I whispered, twirling my hair in tiny spirals.

"Him. The one you've loved. I want to be addicted to you." He paused. "I'm addicted to many things. Cigarettes. When I'm not smoking, I'm chewing Chiclets, also."

I smiled at his precocious attempt to impress me. He lit up a match, and the smoke patterns danced from his cigarette, then in the space above the ashtray. "I'm addicted to the beach," I said. "To the chaffing sand crunching under my feet, tickling my skin. To the washed up shells praying to be scooped up into an open palm…"

"You're also addicted to books," he said. "I love smart girls."

I didn't tell him how I often sat in my father's study and avidly read Corneille and Racine plays, Tintin comic books, and the adventures of Fantômette, the French teen-age crime fighter. I loved the smell of books: musty, inky—earthy, perhaps. It wasn't just the smell of paper. It was that of page-turn sweat, the spilled ingredients hastily swabbed off the pages of my mother's Haitian recipe book. The smell of eagerness and hunger for words. The smell of my world.

"Wanna hear something nerdish?" he asked. "I'm addicted to jigsaw puzzles."

I was a jigsaw puzzle waiting to be solved. The clouds in the sky looked like a lost island. I wished to be alone on that island, with Junior, and show him I could be wild too.

"I want to leave Port-au-Prince," I told him. "I want to go somewhere else—some other town, some other country."

At school, during the rendition of the hymne national, I stood solemn, I listened, I sometimes sang, but when the last notes resonated, I pondered life without a country—a nomadic existence, a self-imposed exile.

"What are you running away from?" he asked, but didn't wait for an answer. He got on his feet and helped me stand up. "What about med school? There's an exchange program in the Dominican Republic," he said. "You're smart—you should look into it." Then he asked again, "Do you want me to kiss you?"

"Don't be corny; just do it if you intend to," I said.

"Do you want me to?"

"How well do you kiss?" I asked with a smile.

He came closer, breathing my air. "I heard you like me."

I smelled the hot sauce on his lips. "I heard you're a player."

"You told Estelle I have dreamy eyes."

He smiled against my neck. His lips covered mine before I could draw a breath, and he tasted of hot sauce. One hand slid up my spine, beneath my braids, while the other one settled low on my back and I pressed against him, rising on tiptoes to return the kiss. It rushed me with something dark and heady.

After the kiss, his lips were wet and red, and hung in a slight smile. We sat on the balcony and listened to the crickets and early nocturnal birds, while the breeze rustled the grapevines. I felt a strange, unexplainable, aching sense of loss.

Outside the windows in my father's study, the light seemed to glow from inside the trees; it spilled out from the leaves as the sun rose, a rich, gold-tinted green.

I found the announcement for the exchange program in a wrinkled Le Matin newspaper on Papa's oak table. Applicants, ages thirteen to eighteen, were invited to submit a 1,300-word essay in Spanish in which they justified their desire to become medical doctors. *We will select the best applicants; these six students will receive a full-year scholarship for a magnet school in the Dominican Republic.* The name of the magnet school had been left out, and so had the name of the sponsoring organization. A phone number was listed, but when Sœur —the better Spanish speaker—dialed the digits, there was no answer.

My sister wore a sleeveless robe of flowing, peach-colored linen. She was turning into a woman.

"Since when do you want to become a doctor?"

"I'm serious about this. That's what I'm meant to be." I had just stepped out of the shower, my body fresh as a hibiscus after a good rain. "Particularly if it means leaving Haiti."

I needed to do something—go somewhere, grow beautiful, have my sorrow drop off me like used-up skin.

She shrugged. "You should ask Maman to stop by, then?" she suggested.

But there was no specific address on the ad.

"I will keep trying," I said.

And I did—the entire day. Once, someone picked up the phone, but all I heard was background noise.

"Hello? Hello?"

No answer.

My face tightened on itself, all line and bone. What I felt was desesperación.

Sœur and I gave up for the day. I sat barefoot on the crimson tiles of the living room to watch Mexican telenovelas and learn Spanish curses, as the crisp mountain air played notes of citrus and woods. Sœur slumped into the couch, laughing, her face twinkly and open. I toppled over onto her, tickled her sides, and my head bounced when she laughed. This game was peaceful, a closer way of laughing together. We were hermanas. We shared un alma.

"I can tell you a scary story," I said when the TV screen went dark after the afternoon blackout.

My sister crouched on her knees in anticipation. It was not the story so much as the afternoon sounds lapping at the open curtains, the room being alive—the house sighed and shuddered, breathing inaudibly through its doors and windows. I began the tale and Sœur fell into it. She leaned in for certain parts, sweaty sunburnt face. She wriggled back through other parts. My voice deepened, and so did the story. The words came from some place deep—they vibrated through the room, wrapped in something ethereal that seemed to convince my one-person audience it wasn't me speaking at all, but the evil character in the story, the man in the yellow raincoat. Sœur sat with her knees up, holding her toes, as we traveled in the lands of giant mabouya and thirsty Cochons-sans-poils.

***

In the car to Estelle's house the next day, I mentioned the exchange program to Mother. Papa eyed me in silence for a moment, hands tight around the steering wheel.

"Santo Domingo?" he said. "You planning to become a prostitute?"

Mother cut in. "There are good med schools in the DR," she said. "I've heard about UNPHU and UCAMAYMA. Sergo's brother attended one of them, didn't he?"

Papa nodded. "Spanish lessons would serve the girls well—but no one is going to Santo Domingo. I heard about that med school Frero attended. A concentration camp. Those dirty panyòl don't like us. There was a curfew for Haitian students—some students almost got shot because they were hanging out in the streets after nine o'clock."

He was making this up as he went. His speech sped up when he lied, and he stressed the end of each sentence. He was un mentiroso—a liar.

"I want to take Spanish lessons," I said.

I figured I might go to the Dominican Republic, after all—Papa might change his mind if I got the scholarship. My brain itched with the possibilities—Spanish lessons, a scholarship, a year in the Dominican Republic. Then—off to somewhere else.

"I saw a pamphlet at school," Sœur said. "For Spanish lessons, I mean."

She'd been reading Prosper Mérimée's *Colomba*; I'd forgotten she was in the car.

"Señora Valles gives private Spanish lessons at her house on Marcadieu Street. We can walk there from Estelle's house and get more information."

"Very well," Papa said.

On the radio, the well-intentioned voices of the announcers reported on the embargo's absurdities, on the unprovoked slaughters. These voices, drained of certainty, caught themselves just short of assertion.

Papa dropped us off for another unsupervised day at Estelle's quaint brick house with the large backyard peppered with several berry trees and thick, dark green moss, where we often spread a blanket for picnic lunches. Flowers bloomed, surrounding the house in red, yellow, purple, blue, and pink. Many times we'd gone exploring and traipsed barefoot through the crunchy, "Oh my god, is that poison ivy?" underbrush.

As the embargo remained and I continued to hang out with Estelle, our friendship became strange—our alliance followed tidal shifts we could neither predict nor chart after the fact. We swore to God to keep secrets we later blurted out. I fell into moods so dark and long and private that Estelle watched from a distance. I lost my train of thought and sat blinking, walled in a thick dissatisfaction. I moved from amusement to irritation and frustration, to suppressed anger, and then amusement again, since my moods vanished without warning.

My shifting mood annoyed Estelle. Like the time she told me Junior was not interested in me. She didn't choose her words like someone who cared; she slapped me with them. "He has a girlfriend," she whispered in that hushed tone she used, when she had a hateful secret to share. She had brown eyes, dark and far apart. Her dog, Snowflakes, was hard of hearing. It was a little thing, but it made me feel better about myself.

Then Estelle was grim with guilt. "Maybe he does care."

Junior—I couldn't imagine the anxiety of being looked at, of being looked into. I was eager for fire, terrified to burn.

Junior's chin was strongly dimpled. He jerked forward with first one wide shoulder, then the other, as though he had to knock down the air to get through it. He held my elbows to kiss me and his lips were chapped, dry as parchment, but sweet. Our lips stamped together like a punch press making something hard and flat. On the phone, Junior had the habit of ending conversations abruptly, with no long prelude or series of false closes. Click, and he was gone.

Sparkly makeup on my eyes and cheeks, I wrapped a leg over the back of his motorcycle, hoisted myself onto the cracked vinyl seat, as the hot air ran its fingers through my hair. Papa would go nuts if he ever saw me on this bike. A murky sensation, compounded of guilt, euphoria and dim apprehension, stirred in me. I tried to imagine what Junior would become in twenty and some years. Would he be a father who hugged and comforted, or a father whose hands hit and terrified? My mind, spurred by a familiar anger, galloped furiously ahead.

At first, I did not allow myself to care about him. But soon love magnified the smallest things—a thin wind across a wire, a single leaf in unsuspecting light, star-shaped, with a pointed lobe, and swaying. Around Junior, I poeticized the waking sun, a squint of sound, a flutter on a branch. Maybe love can save us from the pain in the world. You become so absorbed in the unfoldings and promises and anxieties of love, you have no room to mourn Haiti's terrible suffering. Or your own.

Junior was eighteen, five years older than I was, and he already wore a beard. He lived life with a chattering passion that made me forget people could be wicked, broken, and lost. He spoke of mechanics, of God and Indian spirituality, of computers and hacking techniques, of Kama Sutra and

Bob Marley, of the importance of love and charity. I loved his vitality, his quickness of mind, the twinkle in his eyes when I doubted his love and he called me silly.

He loved jazz and the blues, dreamed of becoming a bassist. On Tuesday nights, he watched jazz bands on TV, belting out swing and bebop solos. On non-school days, he picked us up from Estelle's and we drove to his mother's house in Delmas, where we played cards or dominoes on a table fitted with a green velvet cloth. The guys there looked like gangsters from a mafia movie—poised, dangerous. I watched them smoke cigarettes and drink coconut rum while listening to Junior's Sweet Micky or T-Vice records. One of the guys was Alix, Estelle's boyfriend. His eyes watery and bloodshot, the whites yellowed, he tried to explain the sacred highs of marijuana, the wounded lows, the dead time in between.

On our second date, Junior took me to the hospital to visit his dying grandmother. In the hallways, some people looked dazed, exhausted. Others, elated. A strange exuberance mounted in me: it was the IV needle in her arm, the steady drip of serum, Junior's mother whispering to herself, eyes hazy with pain and glossy with tears. In this room, death breathed down my neck. When I disappeared, it was not like the sky would rip open, or like the stars would lose their way. It never did for anyone else.

I watched all of this as if a stranger to this world.

If I became a doctor, the hospital world, with all its tubes and wires, would become mine. Doctors and nurses rushed around. A patient's pulse raced with a stranger's fresh blood. Nothing stood still. The air riddled with risings and fallings, shifting odds. There is life and there is death. We all die. We all end up as lifeless sacks of flesh. That's just the way it is. I hoped Junior's grandmother had made the most out of her time here.

A doctor.

The possibility had grown on me.

I wanted this.

A skinny man in the hallway struggled with a child who screamed and kicked. The little girl had learned that her mother was dead and she was scratching at the hand that held her tightly by the wrist. The man yelled at the child to stop it, stop it, stop it, yanked her hand, and smacked her. Something about the man, about the meanness in his eyes, struck me. My eyes itched, and I had trouble breathing. My hands shook with the desire to strangle him.

Junior was impervious to my emotions, until I could no longer stop myself and threw the lukewarm content of my coffee mug at the stranger's chest.

"Leave the kid alone," I said with a snarl.

The man was too stricken to react. The child stopped crying.

Junior was horrified, and I felt bad for him, getting tangled up with me. To Junior, I said, "Get used to it," and I meant it. I scrambled around my skull to defend the way I was being. I couldn't quite root out the truth in this, but I sensed some ghost of it hovering.

thirteen

Complaints rose from their bed as I stepped past my parents' door—this bed, where they'd conceived their children, hands searching each other in the dark, coaxing harmony out of hiding. I happened to hear Mother's sigh, Father's deep voice. "You'd better have a talk with your daughter."

"I'm sure she's not dating," Mother said. "She's not even fifteen."

My parents had long lost the rhythm of lovers who have nothing to lose. They were past frustrated shouts that thumped the walls, past threats and accusations, past dramatic pauses, their voices now measured and bored. Papa cranked the radio low in the idling light as Mother put away pairs of pants, and shirts folded in rigid squares, socks balled up like grenades.

Everyday, I called the phone number listed in the newspaper for the exchange program. Nothing. I also perused new issues of *Le Matin*, hoping to stumble upon an updated ad. No luck.

I worked on my essay. In my room, silence tied its knots. It swallowed me and I was suspended in the dark warmth of its throat. Writing allowed me to avoid the world, its endless conversations. I wrote until the gas lamp died, until the night swallowed everything, even an ant crawling across the floor. Outside, the sky wore black rags. I imagined dead men in the barbwire above the walls. They hung on the wires like scarecrows.

I wanted to leave Haiti—the violence, the fear, the rage. In my home and my country.

My past, fanned out flat like a series of cards, would not make the proper sense when turned over.

Mother stopped by Señora Valles' house and got a brochure for the Spanish lessons. Since Sœur and I had been watching Mexican soap operas on Univision, Mother believed we might have a talent for foreign languages. Señora Valles smiled. Her hair, her nose, her chin—they were all short. She spoke rapidly, her large eyes moving with an intent sociability between my mother and me. She took an unashamedly flagrant delight in asking questions.

"Why med school?"

"Hospitals make me feel alive." And I'd come to believe the answer I gave everyone.

Mother looked proud. Everyone in Haiti wished their child a doctor, a lawyer, an engineer.

I had developed a fascination with death itself. Many Haitians shared it on some level. Why else would they walk through old cemeteries and read strangers' headstones? At night, when I unlocked my closet and laid my bone collection[21] on the carpet to study anatomy lessons, a tingle of some restless emotion snaked through my body. A presence both captivating and appalling.

I asked Señora Valles if she'd heard about the exchange program—no, she said with a heavy Castellano accent. I also called Instituto Lope de Vega, another Spanish-language school in Port-au-Prince, and later talked to the Dominican Consulate. They were clueless.

Señora Valles' intensive Spanish lessons took place around a large table in an air-conditioned room.

I'd been going to class for the past three weeks. I was making progress but I was starting to think that I was learning Spanish in vain, that I wouldn't be going to the Dominican Republic.

Someone finally picked up the phone for the exchange program. A man set up an interview with me on the following Monday. "Bring your essay," the voice said. "Ask for Monsieur Gabriel."

"Thank you," I said, short and hot into the mouthpiece, the exhaled breath coming back at me smelling sour.

In the essay, I'd included the fact that I collected human bones. The undertaker's assistant at the city morgue, a man with humongous breakouts on his forehead, sold me the pieces. I boiled them on the makeshift stove in the backyard to take out the gristle and other smelly cartilage still clinging to the bones. I polished them and kept them in my bedroom closet because they made Felicie nervous and I didn't want to scare her.

---

21 Real human skeletons are available for purchase at local hospitals in Haiti. Creepy, I know.

"How did you get these?" Sœur asked one evening, looking for a pink top to match her multicolored shorts.

It had been a breezy, tulip-soft day. The sky had blinked into darkness.

"Junior is resourceful," I said. I showed her a random piece. "They tell me med students in Port-au-Prince keep skeletons at home to help them study. I'm not kidding."

For a long time, I was missing the most important part: the skull. When no one claimed a body, the undertaker's assistant, who happened to be Junior's cousin, buried the head in the backyard of the morgue. "They're the cages of the souls," he said. "They belong to the Baron." Baron Samedi was the gatekeeper of the cemeteries.

One Sunday morning, Junior persuaded an intern to get me a cadaver's head in exchange for movie tickets. "Fear the Baron's anger," the young man warned.

The skull was from a young man who'd died from pneumonia. I was not sure how long ago death had captured his soul. Two teeth remained and green powder covered the bone. I placed the skull in a plastic bag and put it in the closet.

Mother was furious. "C'est de la barbarie!" she said. It's barbarous.

"I want to be a bone doctor," I said. "Remember?"

"An orthopedist, you mean?"

"Yes—that. I have an interview for the exchange program."

"You heard your father. You're not going to the Dominican Republic."

My fixation with the shapes and forms of nature was also about the power in storytelling. I was a goddess. Someone had died and I owned a piece of personal history. Each bone came from a different subject and was reminiscent of a scattered life. I found it fascinating to imagine what the lives of these people had been like. My pelvis was a prostitute on Rue Lamartine. My clavicle—a tonton macoute lynched by the chimères. My sternum—a handsome young man who strangled his unfaithful fiancée and later committed suicide.

At night, I wrote about it.

My life was a deconstructed text, and I was surrounded by words—their sustaining luxuries and dangers. Words have power; you never know what may come of them. Take this: *I want to leave*—the rest is a jigsaw of memory taking up space in my head. *I want to escape to wherever else*. I wrote about what I wanted: to become a doctor, to tell stories, to escape Haiti and my father.

I wanted it all.

Mother wouldn't take me to the interview. Papa wouldn't hear of it.

I decided to sneak out of the house.

Papa was in his room—I could hear the TV and a soccer match. The excitement in my throat made it hurt to swallow. I found myself in a strange body, my own body as it turned out.

When I stepped outside, the world had stopped. The sky was a thick, padded gray, and everything was still and quiet. Felix ate a banana in the vegetable garden. Next to him—a machete, wooden-handled, slightly rusted. The gatekeeper, he needed to let me out. I could see in his eyes that he was wondering where I was going, but he would never dare question the daughter of the house.

He had an uncomfortable giggle. "Be careful; there are thieves out there. Do not trust anyone."

I was too excited to feel dread. My life was taking a new turn, and I didn't want to think about danger.

"Around what time should we expect you back, mademoiselle?" Felix asked. He reached nervously for the Texaco cap on his round head.

I read concern in his eyes, but also something else—the question, What is this crazy, byen-li-twò-byen girl planning now?

I shook my head. "I don't know."

I could see the hunger in him to know the details. It was the storyteller in him: he wanted to know the worst and shudder at it.

It was the longest conversation I'd had with Felix since that one night some October ago when we played basketball. When we leaned against the chicken coop, washed the tomatoes with our spit, and dried them on our soiled shirts.

The iron gate radiated heat. Felix hesitated, the creases on his forehead taut. Then he opened the gate, reminded of my authority over him as one of the ladies of the house. My heart was alive and vibrant, beating with a loud thumpity-thump. I kicked pebbles, walked on an earth-beaten path, surrounded by mountains harboring secrets I yearned to discover, feeling the ancient presence of people who had walked here before me and worked the land. I looked at the patterns of ant-rich trees. I listened to the birds that sang indifferently. A child in an unbuttoned shirt was drawing rusty hills and stick-figure trees on a wall with chalky pieces of slate, his knees covered in gravel.

On the main road, cars whisked by. I stopped in front of Jean-Noel's stand and bought a pack of cigarettes. Two things about Jean-Noel: He grimaced when he talked and he said yes in a singular way, with a huge effort of concentration. I wondered what would happen to him if he ever failed in his effort.

"A pack of cigarettes? Yes."

I'd never smoked before, but maybe in Santo Domingo I would become one of these women who held a cigarette between manicured fingers, looking grave and ageless with an expression that said, "I know life. I've been there." I didn't know the meaning of what was happening to me, but I hoped the force or forces at work were satisfied with my decision to make the appointment despite my parents' refusal.

I bought a lighter and shook one of the Comme Il Faut out. I rolled the cigarette around the palm of my hand and tried right there to light it. The tiny tongue of the lighter felt hard against my thumb and I couldn't manage to create the flame. Jean-Noel's puzzled stare wasn't helping. I kept on trying, until he cleared his throat and said I was too slow. I tried a quicker move and the flame ignited. Holding the cigarette in my mouth, I put the flame against the tip, but I didn't know about inhaling, so nothing happened.

I became aware that a group had formed. Conversation had stopped around the stand, and two kids leaning against Mr. Etienne's house were quiet, their eyes pressed against me. The quenêpe and orange vendors looked at me as well. Girls like me did not walk around alone in town, and didn't stop to buy cigarettes at the corner. Certainly not. Well-brought-up girls didn't smoke, and they rode around in expensive cars.

One of the women broke the silence. "Fòk ou rale sou sigarèt la," she said, her voice surprisingly sweet—a smoky falsetto.

I did what she said, pulling on the cigarette with my breath. Feet away, the freeway quieted and then picked up as if the vehicles traveled in packs. The cigarette tasted like dry grass and I almost choked. One of the kids laughed at my pained expression; the other clapped in excitement. I smiled, remembered to pay for my new acquisitions, and went on walking. On the side of the road, a mutt with a broken leg, a creature of sorrow, rested his head on his front paws. Half-curled, he flashed a tooth and wagged. Then he looked forward.

The kamyonèt that stopped was packed. The driver said, "Hop in the front so you don't get squeezed."

The special treatment. It wasn't the clothes—these were simple jeans and a free promotional t-shirt from the grocery store. It was the color of my skin, a few shades lighter. It was the texture of my hair—maybe not as kinky. I was the tifi wouj, the red girl of Thomassin 38. When I walked around the neighborhood, other kids followed my steps, staring, just like you'd follow a strange animal to study its behavior outside its regular habitat. I tried to befriend some of the children once, and one of them laughed out of surprise: "She speaks Creole!" I was a peculiar species that didn't belong in the streets.

I got in the front of the bus, and the driver turned down the music to ask me whether I was going to Pétion-Ville. I told him yes, but that my final destination was Place d'Italie, in the Bicentenaire, and could he please tell me how to get there? He nodded with a cheerless smile. He wore loose clothes and his hair had started to dread. He smelled of heavy sweat and faint cologne, but the open windows of the bus let in the smell of pine trees and wild flowers, too. The music was blaring again—some Haitian rap. I felt out of place in the overcrowded bus, with people who didn't see me as one of their own. A woman passed on the street; she had wonderful dark skin I would have liked to wrap over myself, over my head.

Skin dark and rich, like Papa's.

The driver yelled at a passenger to throw away his cigarette, goddamnit. He didn't want to get cancer. Then, to save on gas, he shifted to neutral and the bus rolled downhill—a roller coaster ride on a rickety bus. I was getting farther away from home, the bus making stops every two or three blocks, when a potential passenger waved from the side of the road. I started to sweat as the bus got more crowded. I asked the driver if I could smoke and he said, "Of course." He didn't look me in the eyes.

The kamyonèt stopped in Pétion-Ville. The driver explained how to catch a bus to Lalue and then a taxi to Place d'Italie. Teenage boys in the bus talked about an infant who'd nursed its dead mother at the hôpital général and choked when milk turned to blood. They talked about the embargo, pointed fingers at a militaristic government—"the de facto government that American president, Bill Clinton, and his pals are pretending to be punishing for the coup," one of them said—that had easy access to the expensive gasoline while the people could no longer afford bus fares. Daily life in Port-au-Prince was filled with thousand of details that exhausted any energy not already drained by the heat.

The boys warned me against a demonstration downtown. "Don't go to Place d'Italie," one of them told me. "They're protesting the president's return." He had a scar on his forehead; it was shaped like an apostrophe. "The demonstrations have been sporadic since the gas embargo.[22] Today is your unlucky day."

His friends sang in unison: "OEA, OEA, lè m grangou, m pa jwe." They tapped their feet on the bus floor. "OAS, OAS, hungry bellies don't kid around."

I bit my lower lip. "I'm meeting someone there," I said, curling a piece of hair behind my ear.

A woman tucked a baby under her arm like a bread loaf.

The boy with the apostrophe knitted his brows. "Careful. It gets so hot you'll want to take off your skin and walk around in your bones."

---

22 The Organization of American States (OAS), angered and frustrated by the defiance of Haiti's military-backed government, tightened its embargo against Haiti as punishment for its continued failure to end dictatorial rule and permit the return of ousted President Aristide.

Port-au-prince was a miasma of gasoline and diesel fumes mingled with spicy food to create an acrid smell that on a bad day could burn the inside of your nostrils. And I was in the crowd, among strangers, trapped in the web of a giant spider, the air thick with beer, tobacco, hair oil, and Vaseline. Creatures snaked their way between the strands of my hair, slithering worms of sweat wriggling down into my neck.

At Place d'Italie, the sky hung heavy. A group of men surrounded an overturned car and on a corner tires smoldered from recent violence. The demonstration was still going on—behind the barricades, dozens of piétons shouted angrily against Aristide's return, singing *Si Aristide tounen, n ap pran les armes, Seigneur.* The Port-au-Prince sun blazed overhead, the temperature reaching the high nineties; heat radiated from the concrete. Men were leaning against the barricades and burned-down cars—chimères or members of the opposition, I didn't know.

"I need to go through," I said. And I was surprised that I didn't sound afraid.

The men eyed me. "Saw pran se paw," one of them said, and I heard the threat in his voice. "At your own risk."

He let me go through, and I plunged into the sea of demonstrators, avoiding the camera crews. *OEA, OEA, lè m grangou, m pa jwe.* I smelled aftershave: stinging, lively, the musty stench of old clothes and yet another smell: urine and rotted waste. Flies swarmed around the sweat-soaked bodies. I tried my best to avoid the mud that clogged the paved street. Sweat dampened my hairline and glued my clothes to my skin. I passed the brick houses that looked like small jails, the dirty men, the sagging women standing before a half-burned-down house. On the walls were spray-painted the words OEA, pa fè sa. A blan who looked European snapped a pink camera with a fat pink finger.

I reached the address—some kind of office duplex. When I pushed open the slatted doors, coarse laughter welled up from a corner of the room, which reeked of alcohol and stale tobacco and was in the shadows, as if the anger of Port-au-Prince could be trapped on the outside, behind closed windows. Two men and a woman played dominoes, slapping down the pieces in childish glee, black points dotting the poorly-shaven faces of the males. I politely asked the woman for Mr. Gabriel. She smiled, said, "Tout de suite"—right away—and disappeared behind a door.

The sun sewed heat in the room, not with needle and thread, but friction and swish. Sweat trickled a path down my neck, between my breasts. Sticky rivulets ran down beneath my t-shirt, into the waistband of the fabric of my jeans. I ran my tongue along my upper lip; the sun had parched me. I was dizzy from the heat and the stench coming from the street.

"I'm sorry," the woman apologized, returning after a moment. "Mr. Gabriel did not come today. He's back in the Dominican Republic. Maybe next month?"

A chill climbed the knuckles of my spine. I looked out the window—angry men rode in a dusty pickup with the rear doors flung open; they brazenly pointed wooden sticks at the demonstrators. Smoke rose from hills of trash, blanketing the air with a grayish pall. I took it all in: the mosquitoes, the flies, the hot sun, and the rising humidity. The woman kept talking but the words stopped making sense and I didn't pay attention to them. I shook my head to clear the murkiness from my mind, but my dizziness increased. I pressed my forehead against my palm.

I'm stuck here.

When I stepped outside, my vision swam—it was the heat, the dust raised by the wind, the stench of the sewer and of stale urine, and the rage of my emotions. I took in the panorama of ancient wooden buildings, their facades and steep, tile roofs warped by the intense heat. People of all shapes and shades of black stamped their feet on the ground, their faces furrowed and tanned. Under the sun-drenched blue of the sky, the demonstration raged, and the crowd squeezed the breath out of me. Too much old sweat, too many bodies close to mine, too many people breathing down my neck. The crowd bustled and swirled, everyone touching, squeezing, groping. I wanted to be lifted by angels.

On top of a red pick-up in the middle of the crowd, a man with thick glasses and a green hat, draped in the red and blue Haitian flag, yelled to the protesters through a megaphone. "Aristide p ap tounen." Aristide is not coming back! His voice was a rapid-fire staccato.

The sharp crack of gunfire broke his words. "Everyone down!" a startled voice yelled. Another shot. Closer. It cut through the crowd's roar. *Gotta get out of here.* Everyone was on the run, but I was petrified; I couldn't move. My heart was pounding, and I couldn't breathe. Men wearing bandanas above their mouths and clutching automatic weapons were getting closer. My knees went weak.

Someone grabbed me from behind. I didn't scream. Lost in the nightmare, fear pumped through my veins. "Get behind here," a man said as he pulled me down behind a gigantic trash can. "You'll be safe."

His voice was calm, different from the one that screamed in my head for the nightmare to stop. I gagged at the stench from the waste; the ground was puke green. As I lay in the mud, I heard more screaming. I pulled my knees to my chest and wrapped my arms around my calves, trembling. But in the midst of this, the sky remained a beautiful blue. A dog barked somewhere in the distance. I didn't want to die. The man lay behind me, and I felt his breath on my neck.

Was anyone dying out there? My stomach rumbled. My heart beat in my ears. A rat ran past my nose.

The chimères—or whoever—were gone. My knees were wobbly as the man helped me stand, and my heart beat in my throat. I inhaled a quick, gasping breath. I didn't brush the dirt and gravel off my jeans. A woman was screaming; a bullet had hit her in the leg, and her blood swirled in patterns on the pavement. I was too terrified to help. A man with a chin beard pulled her up, into a kamyonèt. I clamped my hand over my mouth to kill the scream in my throat.

"Where are you going?" a man asked. He was the one who had rescued me. He was lean and bony, and ropy veins stood out on his neck and forearm. I couldn't tell his age. Somewhere between twenty and fifty. He looked like a boy in a man's skin. A slight man, no fat on his body.

"Thomassin," I said. My head was still woozy and my stomach churned. The heat made it worse.

"I'll get you there. Vini."

I searched his face. It was not the face of a man with ulterior motives. It was just a face, stretched by smiles. Later, I would remember the careful driving of the Good Samaritan. He didn't gun his Datsun through the potholes like the cowboys who usually drove around Port-au-Prince, whooping as they left the ground, ruining the shocks and having a good time doing it. He drove at a sedate speed—with an Old World dignity.

In the yard, Felix held a dead chicken in his grip, and drops of blood trickled down onto his bare foot. On the balcony, Mother mopped damp hair from her face with the back of her forearm and unsettled a gang of mosquitoes. She leaned back and pulled her legs up onto the chaise longue. The sunlight played on her face and her eyes blinked.

"What happened to you?" she asked.

"I was walking in the neighborhood; I fell in the mud."

My parents thought I'd been writing in my room. I found my father slouched on a canapé, a clean white handkerchief peeking from the pocket of his shirt, today's *Le Nouvelliste* in his hands. He saw me, and delight crinkled the skin at the corners of his eyes. How far apart we'd grown. I was no longer the child who folded myself into my father's lap, his chin resting on top of my head, his newspaper folded the same way he folded it every day.

He smiled and took my hand in his, "Est-ce que tu aimes ton Papa?" And even though I didn't answer the question and took my hand away, he looked at me as if there were a bond between us, as if we understood each other. Sweat had turned clammy inside my shirt. I wiped away the fat drops that gathered in furrows on my forehead, crowned my brow, and glistened on my nose. The clock ticked loudly, clicking off each second with a jump.

fourteen

Junior put his hand in the small of my back and leaned into me. He strummed a few chords, tuned his guitar, and launched into a song by Serge Gainsbourg. *Couleur Café. Que j'aime ta couleur café.* His voice was deep and thrilling, lifting and meeting the wind, his expression solemn. His eyes, tidy black seeds, settled on me.

Junior and I shared strange hobbies, like taking rides to Thomassin's graveyard. When the tires crunched on the rocky road, salty dust in a lazy tornado around the car, we smiled. We listened to the last verse of the song and waited for the dust to settle. "This is good. This is so good." Our doors opened and slammed in tandem. Cemeteries and rites of passage fascinated Junior; he told me stories about the Jews who do not eat meat, drink wine, or shave for the first week after a death; when a Hindu dies, the family makes offerings of rice balls and milk at a shrine for the next ten days. Muslims read the Qur'an for forty days after a death in the family, and the Tiwi people of Bathurst Island use body paint as a disguise so the dead will not recognize anyone and take their friends and family with them.

Listening to his stories, I took in the fresh perfume of oranges and eucalyptus that filled the air of the cemetery. The sky was clear. Junior smelled of gin, menthol cigarettes, lavender, and sweat. In the car, his hand brushed against my breast; almost accidentally, but lingering half a second too long for it not to be deliberate.

"Is going to the Dominican Republic down the drain?" Junior asked.

I sighed. "I guess."

He hesitated. "What about the United States, the land of the free?" He paused. "I know a man."

"What man?" I asked.

"Alix's brother. From Santo Domingo, he gets people to the United States—for a fee. He has the right—resources."

"Isn't that risky?"

Junior held his unlit cigarette like he would a syringe and tapped on it with his middle finger. "Of course. What do you think?"

The week before, the police had closed off Rue du Centre and arrested a dozen forgers—they'd given up the list of their clients. Rue du Centre was the Mecca for fake American documents. It was the place; it was the spot. Sweeping the area, though, only got rid of those who were easily replicable, and the lowest in the operation.

"The head of the operation has moved to Santo Domingo," Junior said.

He was speaking to me, but I felt what he was saying was something I shouldn't hear, as though he was talking to himself, not realizing I was still here. But then he asked, "How badly do you want to leave?"

I looked upward—at the stars, at their light twinkling in the dusk. A hazy butterfly wriggled, itched, and squirmed, making circles out of figure eights, before it disappeared. I imagined U.S. soldiers surrounding Alix's house, torturing him to get the names of his brother's clients. I shivered. Too risky.

"I'm not sure," I said.

"Keep it in mind. We could leave together."

When we went back to his house, Junior's mother was on the patio, wearing a muumuu and a straw hat, speaking to herself before she spotted me and laughed hard and sang and laughed again and threw a spaghetti plate at Junior.

Junior said his mother was tèt pa byen, sick in the head. Maybe schizophrenic. She hadn't officially been diagnosed. Most in Haiti hadn't.

"I'm driving her to Jimani in a few days," Junior said, after I'd helped him clean up. "She's not dealing well with Grandma being in the hospital. Her side of the family is from the Dominican Republic. Her sisters will take care of her." He looked grave. "I'm afraid I'm like her and simply don't know it."

"Me too."

"What?" He was confused.

"I mean—I'm afraid I'll end up like my father."

His mother had persistent hallucinations. She saw madansara birds in an empty sky or heard a nonexistent ringing telephone, so that in the middle of a silent stretch she suddenly looked up and said, "Aren't you going to get that?" She'd invented a bourik that lay at the end of Junior's bed but didn't like to be petted by anyone but her. There was also some mildly delusional thinking. She thought she was allergic to certain words, and if anyone said them in her presence, she believed she was breaking out in a rash. The words had to do with medical terminology—nurse, doctor, blood, needle.

"Being in Jimani will soothe her," Junior said. He added, looking grave, "I wish you would come with me."

The night was flustered and furrowed, the clouds like bruised plums. When sleep wouldn't find me, I opened the phone book and put my finger down on any page, any number. I woke strangers and talked to them. Many cursed and hung up. Others listened considerately, until I was ready to fall asleep.

And when I woke up from my nightmares, it was morning. I shifted in bed, stretching my stiffness like a skin I was pushing out of.

Screams came from downstairs.

"Mind your damned business."

The shrill voice of Papa.

I imagined the finely combed hairs of his upper lip bunched up and twitching under his anger. Papa's mood swings turned me in circles so that I no longer knew where it was in this world I was supposed to hide. He was breaking me. He was angry and I was eager for peace. His changes were like the motion of the moon: one night a crescent cupped gently like an open hand, the next, a round flat iron skillet.

It was Monday—the schools were closed because of the embargo.

"Stop shouting," Felicie said in a measured tone.

I scurried down the steps in my bare feet and found Felicie stooping over the sink, rattling dishes as she handled the soggy dishrag with her knotted fingers. Papa's eyes were bulging, his mouth set. He plopped his plate in without bothering to rake the last forkful of rice into the trash can first, reaching in front of Felicie to rinse his big, square hands.

"Get out of my house," Papa told her. He squinted his eyes into slits, frowning until his jowls seemed ready to slide off his face.

I narrowed my eyes as I felt the familiar caving-in of my chest. *No, no, no. Not Felicie!*

The sight of him fueled ire in me. It was a dry, parched anger. My body flattened, and if they cut me open they'd find the Sahara. He didn't do anything right. Loser dad, loser husband. But I had a new rule: quiet and inertia. Because what if a ripple swelled a catastrophe? I was not about to shed a tear.

Felicie wrinkled her forehead and pursed her mouth, forming lines on her top lip like cat whiskers. She continued washing dishes with jerky movements, coming as close to tossing them as she could without shattering the glass. Papa glanced at her; she stared into the gray sudsy water. Papa grunted and twitched his shoulders. When he slammed the door of his study, the house shook like a disturbed bird squawking and ruffling its feathers. I looked down at the table strewn with a dissected newspaper, a plate of crumbs, coffee cups, a stack of napkins, a sugar bowl. A family table, with the ordinary objects a family shared.

Felicie dried her hands then looked stiffly around the kitchen, as if someone had run off with the cabinets. Her eyes were narrowed by sheer sadness. "I'll be going," she said.

I let out the breath I didn't know I'd been holding. "He didn't mean it," I said.

She frowned. "You know he did."

I changed into an ironed shirt that itched at the collar. Felicie and I walked the dusty, rutted road together. Women with wrinkled brown faces called to me, ignoring Felicie. Bèl tifi wouj, they said. Bèl tifi, come here, come to see what I have to offer. What they had to offer was this: beef and pork and lamb, freshly slaughtered, eggs in baskets, piles of peppers, tomatoes, and watermelons stacked on emptied bags. The sun pacing the lighted sky was warm on my neck. The shadows had tilted away, away, and my clothes stretched out with perspiration.

"What are you going to do?" I asked.

She was old—ancient. "I'll be okay. It won't be the first time an old maid got fired."

"I hate him."

We passed the fields of corn, green stalks like lizard skin. I ran my tongue between my lip and my upper teeth, slipped in and out between the gaps. My breath was sour, my teeth unbrushed.

"What happened? Why was he so mad?"

She smiled a sad smile. "You know your Papa—he loves the drama. When his life gets too dull, he adds his own spices—often poisonous." She shook her head, the sad smile not leaving her face. "I don't believe he can help it."

"Will I see you?" I asked.

"Of course, you will."

But her tone was uncertain, and I was getting a headache.

A kamyonèt stopped. Skinny and tattooed goats hung upside down, next to machetes that would later slice their heads. And chickens—silent. The driver's face had a scar running down his cheek, and he stared at us with ravenous intensity.

Mother was still at church—a special service on that Monday morning. Sœur had once called her a "terrible mother" for putting up with Papa. But to me, she was a mother who, despite everything, bestowed necessary mercies, alleviated the night-burning fevers of her children. She'd be struck when she got home and found Felicie gone, but I wouldn't be there to see it.

That was it. I was going to escape to the Dominican Republic with Junior, to Jimani where his grandfather still owned a small spaghetti factory and a bakery. Junior was leaving with his mother; I was sure he'd still be willing to take me along for the ride.

I'd run away. Leave it all behind. Maybe the past would then fade—decline.

When Junior called, hours later, I meant to tell him about my plans to escape, but I worried Papa might be listening. Plus I didn't want my pain and fear to cast him off. I imagined his kiss, a slow desperation, his tongue and lips, soft and sweet.

"What about Jimani?" I asked casually, my eyes on the gravel road outside my window, on the lengthening shadows, the neighbor's undergarments and sheets hung out to dry. Babies cried in one of the apartments next door, and street dogs fought.

"I'm leaving the day after tomorrow," Junior said. "You would love it, on the other side of the border. We have a pool."

He told me how his mother sometimes stood naked in the pool's shallow end, lifting one leg then the other, twisting at her waist, splashing her face with water and smoothing her silver hair. "She's happy there," Junior said.

A long silence followed.

When Junior hung up, I grabbed my Adidas bag and started packing jeans and t-shirts. I ran a hand over the fabric of the clothes on wooden hangers; I buried my face in my dresses and neatly folded sweaters. I held a flowered blouse to my face and smelled it. I wondered if the clothes that stayed behind would always carry my smell, or if eventually my scent would fade away. Somehow I couldn't bear the thought of it.

I took *Vingt-Mille Lieues Sous Les Mers* from my personal library because I always meant to read something by Jules Vernes. I tucked my writing journal among my panties and bras. I'd been writing a lot lately—falling into tales as into a deep well where no voice could reach me, escaping from the world around me, every breath a story. Sometimes ideas rushed like torrents, poured like rain, saturated my mind, seeped, set, washed away. At other times, my thoughts only quivered, like air full of dragonflies, shuddering all ways, here to there, everywhere yet nowhere—they flashed and twinkled away.

Someone outside was banging on something with a hammer. Toothbrush and toothpaste? Check.

Pictures? I looked through the albums, for what I imagined would be the last time. Some of the pictures of my father were blurred, in half light, or otherwise indistinct. Others were still sharp. I was drawn by the shape of his face, the eyebrows, dark, thin, and arching, the eyes, the lips. I could see my reflection in the vanity mirror. As I faced the mirror, I saw Papa's face. But if I turned to the left, I found Mother. They both stared at me from my own face. Now my skin was breaking out in brown pimples.

Junior said that if you stared at a photograph long enough, it fluttered, and eyes inside nearly winked.

I packed my favorite picture with Sœur. We sat Indian style, holding hands and trying to read each other's minds. The composition of the picture, rich and deep, accentuated and dramatized the image. Dressed alike, right down to our bracelets, necklaces, socks, and shoes, we were positioned oddly within the space, Sœur's arm cut off by the frame of the camera.

It was the only picture I took.

Because I had to tell somebody I was running away, I knocked on Sœur's door. The curtains were drawn and the lights off; the room was dark and heavy. The darkness ebbed in some places and flowed in others and the walls melted together. From the stillness came the rustling and the slapping of sheets and I realized Sœur had been reading in the dark, her eyes adjusting to the obscurity like those of a cat. When I turned on the dim light of her bed lamp, she looked thin in her muumuu. Her luxuriant hair, black and curly, rioted around her delicate head and her eyes were puffy. She'd been crying over Papa's fight with Felicie.

"She is gone," I said.

Her upper lip curled in disgust. She brushed the page of the book, pointer finger holding her place in the tale.

"I'm leaving," I said. "I'm going to the Dominican Republic. I'm not coming back to this house. I'll crash at Junior's place until I know exactly what is what." I leaned against the wall, next to an almanac featuring a smiling Gerber baby. "You have to understand—I'll get as crazy as he is if I stay."

"Okay," she said, raising her elbows as if I were simply asking to borrow her Secret deodorant.

"I'm doing this." The thought of staying in Haiti, the force of it, hit me afresh, hard, not only in my gut but in my chest, my joints, my throat.

"You're thirteen, for chrissake." She snapped. "Leave me alone."

I kissed her on the cheek. I wanted to be out of here before Mother came back from church. Even Sœur seemed other today—outside of me, outside of my kind, which was a thing I couldn't define so much as feel, a set-apartness.

The world gets so big so fast that one can shrink and fall through the cracks like an ant.

I made myself two peanut butter sandwiches.

Soon I was in a kamyonèt, surrounded by the smell of vinyl. The driver tapped his brakes frequently, and it made me sick in my stomach to look at the green swerve of the world I couldn't come out of. In some places, the road was patched with tar and smooth as glass, and the kamyonèt flew until we hit the gravelly asphalt that chattered my teeth.

How easy it had been to pack everything and leave Thomassin—a place that both held me and pushed me away, a place that suffocated with tension and confusion with Papa running in and out of rooms, up and down the stairs. I was running away, escaping to wherever else. Could I say it to the driver? I wanted to speak the words aloud to someone.

The sun lit the pasture across the road, the hills beyond, and I already missed the rattling black typewriter, my stories and poems shining with such promise they sometimes reduced Sœur to tears. Mother fixing my hair as I sat on the plush, comfortable chair with wheels, next to the hundreds of cassettes my father stockpiled. I wondered if Mother, holding a comb, would remember my hair not quite the color of hers. As a child, I thought my hair would eventually grow long, cover my eyes, my breasts, my bones.

I hadn't planned the escape, but I was glad to force fate. The wind bore through me. The ride might end with a tragedy—a killing or a kidnapping, my mouth stuffed with a dirty sock, and while each of the individual risks could tear a hole in my gut, the broad danger anesthetized me. By taking the kamyonèt, I had reduced my options to the point where I felt comforted by the one thing I could do. I could run away.

When I got to Junior's house, a large dog came snapping at me from the other side of the gate, one eye half-closed from some long-forgotten injury; there were lumps on his body, cysts of some sort. A sudden weakness took me, as if my muscles had turned liquid. A woman rushed out of the front door and grabbed the dog by the collar, dragging it to the backyard.

In the front yard, Junior wore a pair of blue jeans—ironed, I could tell by the sharp creases—and a t-shirt, also ironed, starched and tucked in. He had his pack of Comme Il Faut crumpled up in his hand and he shook one into his mouth and lit it, all one smooth motion. His face was raw with scrapes and cuts that obscured his sharply square features. A trail of bruises ran down one cheek and onto his neck.

"God, Junior. What happened to you?"

I watched the muscles of his face freeze one by one—his cheek, his lips, his jaw, his eyebrows. Junior let a line of smoke out the side of his mouth. A loud crash came from inside the house. Junior's eyes were almost hidden by the scowl pressing down on them, and he motioned his chin in the house's direction. "My mother is trashing the place," he said.

We stood silently facing each other, breathing in sweat. Then he stared at his stretched-out arm. His gaze traveled down the length of it, to his wrist, his fingers. I stared at Junior staring at his hand. I couldn't find the words to talk to him.

"What are you doing here?" he asked. Perspiration glittered on his forehead. "Don't tell me. I can't deal with you. Not now, not ever." The unsaid hung in the air, a buzzard, waiting to move in. "Last thing anyone needs is to be dragged into your bummer," he said. "I need you to leave me alone. Go home."

I barely recognized him. His face had a meanness to it; it belonged to a man I knew nothing about. I was filled with a wild mixture of sorrow, regret, empathy, and inexhaustible longing. A breeze came up, one of those phantom things from out of nowhere, and blew some seeds down from an acacia tree.

As the sun came down, the bowl of the sky filled with a dark blue. Palms creaked in the night breeze that blew the smell of night crawlers and lady-of-the-night; their fronds rubbed against each other as though whispering secrets. A large moon settled a silvery blanket of light over the garden. Rats squeaked and rustled among the dry weeds as they went after the empty coconuts. The coqui frogs made their calls and I smelled the bougainvillea flowers and the rotting breadfruit on the night air.

Sœur let me sleep in her bed, relieved I'd come back—but not surprised. Mother came into the room for the night prayer. Jésus, Marie, Joseph, je vous donne mon coeur, mon âme, mon esprit et ma vie. Mother's arms were slightly raised, fingers unfurled, like she was trying not to fall. She looked placid as if on the edge of eternal sleep. On the wall, Jesus followed her gestures with his dark eyes, ready to weep real tears. I took out the rosary beads Papa had given me for my first communion. I liked to feel the beads shift across my palms, their calibrated slither against my skin as I prayed. It was more like a conversation than a prayer.

I curled up around Sœur's back and hugged her close as my mother whispered a lullaby—soft vowels, papery voice—as if we were still small children. She sat on the edge of our bed and read us the French translation of a poem by Wordsworth, "I wandered lonely as a cloud." She kissed our foreheads, lingered at the door to say good night. Then the quiet came.

fifteen

Junior's car crashed on his way to Jimani and he was killed.

Junior—who'd come along and pieced me together by showing me what the future could be like. He'd given pieces of myself back to me, helped me shed the parts that didn't matter. But he was gone and I wanted to be put on fire: orange shapes that'd flicker and deepen in color, ashes billowing with fury. I imagined blowing on a flame, harder and harder, until it became a conflagration that swallowed the world. I missed the staccato rhythm of our talks, his lips brushing against my face, to the side of my mouth, leaving a small, wet place.

After he was gone, there were late nights of perplexity and private sorrow, when I gorged on my own heart, unable to silence my demons. He invaded my dreams, which scattered me across the globe. Junior hid in the corners of my mind and appeared when I was alone—broody, soulful, layers of sweat and oil thickened on his skin like glaze.

And Papa hugged me.

He reached out for me, held me so tight against his chest that he melted into my sorrow with me. And something in my chest tore apart—something grown over, tangled, uncared for.

At the viewing at Pax Villa, in Turgeau, his mother blamed Alix and she had to be restrained, pulled away by her other sons, physically lifted off the ground, her feet moving in mysterious ways. Oh, God, the estranged father cried. Oh, God!

Women screamed, shook, went into convulsions, and dropped to the ground. About six people had to be carried out the side door of the church after they'd fainted from grief.

"Junior talked about you," one of the brothers told me. "You want to be a doctor, don't you?"

"I do." My throat hurt, dry in a place my tongue couldn't reach, an ache outside myself, on the top where ridges calmed down.

The brother slumped over the armchair and peered at everyone from beneath the low visor of his hand. "He was proud of you," he said. "Good luck with med school."

After the mass, the brass band played solemn dirges with silver and gold instruments that glinted in the sun. The musicians, in dark pants, white shirts, dark ties and caps, moved in a slow procession, trailed by two limousines and the crowd of mourners.

Junior's brothers and I followed the long walkway in the cemetery lined with painted crypts. Small houses built above ground. Some topped with crosses, others with rusting padlocks hanging from their hatches. People in Port-au-Prince built big, solid tombs, for fear that if the tombs were not strong enough, evil spirits would enter them and turn the dead into zombies.

Junior loved cemeteries.

Women danced for the spirits—dances full of opposites, subtle and dynamic, graceful and ragged, the vibrant tones and rhythms of the drums creating calm, balance, sensuality, and passion. I watched these women shake, wail, and swoon, go into a trance, shout to the gods, faint and drop to the ground. Some kids played in the cemetery, happily splattered with mud. I heard death's whisper among the coconut trees. The rows of stones stared at me in the breeze. Saints and sinners were buried in adjacent plots of land.

When Papa picked me up, he smiled a sad smile, and I could see a story there—beginning, middle, and ending all laid out within the curves of his mouth.

"Are you okay?" he asked, his words measured.

The longer I stared, the less his face was that of a stranger.

On Career Day, I told my biology teacher I wanted to be a doctor.

"Very well," Madame Cadeau said. "You can write your research paper about one of the branches of medicine."

That night, when I called my uncle Adou for advice, he told me to come by the teaching hospital the next day. I'd get to see an autopsy.

The hôpital général was in downtown Port-au-Prince, where garbage rotted in mounds along the sidewalks. Schoolboys hiked up their pants to jump puddles. Girls in tight braids, crisp corsages and knee-length skirts held hands, their faces freshly scrubbed. There were people everywhere, and cracked asphalt, and gray concrete walls. Pate kòde vendors chased away flies in the repressive heat, and fresko merchants pushed their colorful carts.

"Here we are," Mother said. "Remember, I'm picking you up in two hours."

I smiled. "Maman, you're so cool." I still couldn't believe she was allowing me to skip classes to watch an autopsy.

"I'm glad you're thinking about med school," she said. "I was afraid you were considering poetry or something."

The way she said it, *poetry* sounded like a nasty disease. But it didn't matter to me.

An elderly gentleman dozed in the entryway with a shotgun balanced on his thighs. Mother honked, and the security guard started from his nap. He nodded at Mother and let the car through the parking lot.

The hospital was old, decrepit. In place of the faintly sweet smell of disinfectant, the air hung heavy with the odor of a slaughterhouse. There was a waiting room inside, but the wait line spilled onto the front yard. Patients lay on straw mats or leaned against the concrete building, sweltering in the tropical heat. Women mumbled incoherently or wept, hands pressed to their faces, tears running between crooked, callused knuckles. Next to the admissions office, the body of a man was parked in a wheelchair, the head fallen back, as flies buzzed about. Was he dead? Every day, a bullet. Every day, a body.

I wore old jeans and running shoes. Uncle Adou waited for me in the parking lot, white coat over blue shirt and imprinted red tie. He handed me a lab coat, and gestured with one hand, "In there."

The pungent smell of formaldehyde took me aback and I concentrated on not breathing through my nose. I braced myself for gruesome sights. We passed in front of a huge door, and Adou said that was where they kept the dead. There were bodies in the hallway of the quiet building—a teenager lying in fetal position, as if in sleep; a baby so tiny, she was kept in a shoebox and wrapped in a Ziploc bag. I remembered Junior, then, and the moment his body must have gone limp. The longer I thought about it, the harder it was to imagine him in any way other than this one: laughing—a joint the size of a sausage hanging from his bottom lip, a fragrant pillow of marijuana smoke hanging above his head.

The autopsy room was not what I'd imagined. It was not large nor was it brightly lit. The open windows let in the lemony sun, the sweltering heat, and the dust stirred up from the nearby street. Five medical students stood around a body, chatting softly, as if afraid to awaken the dead covered with a white sheet; they wore hip-length white coats over their skirts and heels, dress shirts and ties. I couldn't wait to wear my own med student attire. I imagined it empowering.

Adou asked, "Ready to start?"

They nodded silently and I held my breath as he whisked away the sheet. My jaw tightened, the saliva pooled behind my teeth.

She was a skinny woman in her thirties who'd had a heart attack. She was almost purple, with dark hair, and her mouth and eyes were open wide, horror crystallized by rigor mortis. A name tag hung from a cord laced around her big toe. Her name was Mireille. Nausea crawled up my throat, but I had to be tough.

Adou examined Mireille's limbs and the outside of her body, and one of the students recorded my uncle's observations into a microphone. Adou's hands were beautiful, and the way he bent his wrist was beautiful, and the way he used the stylus as a scalpel to open the rib cage and peel back the skin. In the fluorescent light, the ribs reminded me of the racks of pork ribs Mother bought at Epicerie de Lourdes. There was little blood. Blood was life. Corpses didn't bleed. Mireille was dead. A student wiped the sweat from his brow. Another raised a handkerchief up to her nose. She spoke to Adou without looking over to where he stood by the corpse.

Each organ was fascinating. The form and function of our anatomy amazed me. I was determined to betray no shock or revulsion. But the image of her body, or of my own self in that state, would haunt me at times afterwards. I pondered what a gift life is, what a difference a single moment makes, how days before, Junior had been very much alive, how sudden his death had been—no time for "I love you," kisses, "I'm sorry," or "goodbye." A sense of validation and thankfulness arose because of the frantic beating of my own heart.

My uncle finally pulled the white sheet back over Mireille. The students left. In a few years I'd be one of them, learning anatomy from gigantic books, tracing complicated drawings of veins and muscles.

"Want to see the morgue?" Adou asked.

How many had died today? At sunup in Haiti, schoolchildren held the promise of a brighter future as they stepped from home to street. At sundown, the rumors started and all the mothers and fathers and aunts and uncles rushed into the streets and called down the narrow alleys: Gaspard! Jean! Amélie! Had anybody been lost today?

The tiny freezer had no fancy drawers—only shelves. The morgue didn't always have electricity, and bodies overflowed, devoured out of recognition by maggots. Dead infants lay stacked in a pile. Babies. So many. "All these babies," I whispered. Masses of decaying flesh, greenish black, they were barely recognizable as humans. I'd heard it on the radio: the oil embargo and the other sanctions designed to help restore democracy to Haiti were killing children.[23]

"Why aren't they cremated?"

"No cremator here. They will be buried in the fausse commune, if no one claims them."

A table with wheels stood in the middle of the room, with a mulatto man in his underwear, arms outspread, yellow face streaked with dried blood, his chest a mess of smashed bones and meat. Huge chunks of ice were scattered around the body to slow decomposition. "It's Mr. Valcin," Adou said. "His daughter Lola is in your class, isn't she?"

She was.

Oh Lord, I hope Lola hasn't seen him like this.

I was disturbed by my sudden, uncanny awareness of death—so absolute, insidious, and cynical—and the oblivion that followed it. However loved, the man on the slab remained forgettable, a drop in the crowded bucket—only inauthentic and deceptive images would remain. Since Junior had died, I couldn't picture his face. I remembered what he did and said but I couldn't remember his face. I remembered his high school graduation picture. He looked nothing like that picture.

"What happened?" I asked. My lips quivered.

Adou said Mr. Valcin had been killed in the morning with a machete. And Lola didn't know yet.

And my hands itched. An uncontrollable itch—as unacceptable as the laughter born in the morbid silence of a funeral, the vibrate-my-body laughter that spread like a virus without a cure, and ran down your cheeks in taunting tears.

And my stomach stirred.

That's when I threw up on my lab coat and tennis shoes. And I was crying, snotting, and hiccupping, now horrified by the strange corpses around me.

I ran outside, in the streets of Port-au-Prince, away from the hospital, until I reached the plaza and the Palais National. I wanted to inhale fresh, cool air and sense it rushing through my body, purifying it. But instead, garbage smelled pungent and rotten and warm.

---

23 The *Economist* and the *Washington Post* both reported that the effects of the embargo on human rights were brutal. The sanctions contributed to extensive malnutrition, disease, and famine. Scarcity of transportation and lack of electricity led to deaths—deaths that could have been otherwise prevented—particularly because vaccines could not be adequately refrigerated or shipped. Children's death rates were twenty times the usual rate. The children died from treatable maladies, such as measles and other commonly treatable viruses.

sixteen

My parents found balance for a while. No more cathartic shouting and storming off into the night or the morning, no more slapped cheeks or shaken shoulders, no more spilled wine blossoming into a purple stain. There wasn't forgiveness either, or certainty that the truce would last. They focused on the routines of domesticity—the hush of a broom, the turning of fans on full blast, the sliding of floss between the cracks of teeth, the fluff of pillows.

Papa and I fought, made up, fought even harder. At times I had a sweet, timid disposition; then suddenly I was combative and quick to anger. Even my body had trouble deciding which shape best suited me. For a few weeks, I was heavy, my belly stretching my bell-bottom jeans. Then one day I fit in my old clothes again; I remained thin for a time, no matter what I ate.

I wanted to go to a nightclub for the first time. I imagined dirty neon lights dangling from ceiling beams; they flickered on and off without rhythm, their wriggly wires crooked like chicken bones strung together on a string. I could almost hear the music in my chest, vibrating, waiting, a wave that would flatten my thoughts, wash them away with a mindless, insistent staccato. I wanted to become part of the pulse of this music—as it pulled me out of myself with a heightened sense of abandon, unreality. I could see it all: on the dance floor, unhooked pelvises, butts that pivoted around their axes. Cocktail stirrers everywhere, like a discarded game of Pick-Up Sticks.

But Papa wouldn't hear of it. *No, you're not going clubbing. For chrissake, you're a kid.* And the conversation had ended with fists and voices raised, doors slamming.

I sat in my father's chair—a tattered and tired office chair I'd lugged to the porch. It showed its age: scarred faux leather, armrests sprouting prickly stuffing, scents of Papa in the fabric. Half shaded by an acacia tree, I sipped rich, dark café au lait, splashing a bit on the ground first, like Felicie used to do, to feed our ancestors. The air was soft with breeze and sweet with roasting coffee, the clouds in the sky moving like fishing boats out on the Caribbean Sea. The voices of the neighborhood rose and fell in spurts. Outside the prisonlike gates of my parents' house in Thomassin, young girls balanced buckets atop their heads, up and down the graveled roads. Sun-wrinkled women sold mangoes and homemade peanut brittle, while boys in cutoff jeans ran in circles with makeshift kites or pushed around trucks made from plastic bottles.

Papa strutted from the house. This angled face was also mine. Only distance made it seem less familiar. My father's hair was still wet from the shower. His I-am-home clothing was worn and comfortable: a stretched-out sweater, blue chinos, and old wool socks. The skin crawled on the back of my neck and the pit of my stomach crashed into my pelvis. My father was more of a jailer than a father. I didn't like his grim outlook on the world and the way he tried so hard to make a father and daughter out of us when we were strangers.

He walked around behind me in his cramped, thin shoes, placed his hands on the back of the chair, and asked, "What are you doing?"

I couldn't see his face but I knew his eyebrows were furrowed in curiosity. I took a deep breath, pushed my wild furious loathing into a place inside myself, and I swallowed. "Thinking," I said.

He sat in the rocking chair next to me, elbows on knees, with his whiskered chin in the palms of his hands, and sighed. He picked up the magazine I'd been reading, clutched it in his calloused hands. "A girl doesn't belong in a nightclub until she's eighteen," he said.

I nodded my head, pretending to be interested.

Papa looked at me. "You don't like me much, do you?"

I raised my shoulders in annoyance. "Don't be ridiculous."

He took a deep breath. He resented the stranger in me. I felt his sadness, the way he slumped over the arm of the chair. He'd been trying extra hard to be in my good graces. He'd brought me books that filled up the ten shelves in my bedroom—the collection of *L'Encyclopedie de la Jeunesse*. The twelve tomes of *La Santé pour Tous*. I read with an intensity that frightened my mother. I made a tent of my yellow ruffled bedspread and read by flashlight, my black cat Slobodan curled on my chest.

But any attempt on my father's part to be friendly with me came across as forced and made me uncomfortable. Except this time: "What if I let you go out with your friends tonight?"

Just like that.

Lakoup Nightclub was crowded, noisy, and literally vibrating with the beat of music blasting through large speakers. The air itself was alive with energy, the crowd abuzz with anticipation. I walked into the music, into the shadows, and the sticky night pressed against my skin until perspiration bead my upper lip. People lined up three deep at the bar, in the rez-de-chaussée of the old gingerbread house. The bartender chatted with a woman. "What is so dreadful about your hair that someone would call it dreadlocks?" she asked.

I didn't know the number of gourdes required for a Coca-Cola or a Prestige beer. I let the sexy bartender get me a cocktail "on the house." I explored the dark, empty rooms upstairs. I walked out on the balcony, the den of iniquity, where a couple smoked weed. The girl laughed and reached up. She slipped her hand under the boy's blue shirt, up near the collar. Her hand moved, rubbing the boy's neck. They wanted privacy, so they left, and I sipped my cocktail, alone under the stars, watching people dancing in the yard.

From the balcony, I saw the band playing in the backyard. Lead singer Michel Martelly's voice was strong and unlabored even when reaching for notes in the upper registers. I loved the grainy vocal quality that lent the band a tortured but familiar sound, as if one were remembering a bad day. Listeners hung on every phrase, awaiting the next pause or streak or curve.

"Hello," a voice said behind me.

There was something boyish about the lanky mulatto standing there—the dimples and the apple cheeks. His hair was wild and shaggy, as if the wind had been playing with it. He was in his late twenties, handsome, with broad shoulders and a narrow waist.

"Do you want to dance?" he asked.

His name was Ben. As he moved me around in a circle, Michel Martelly[24] sang, *Yon samdi swa nan lakou Lakoup, desten fè de moun kontre*. On a Saturday night, at Lakoup Nightclub, their destinies intertwined. The singer laughed and added to the lyrics, "But he was a mad, mad man." Ben's hands left damp spots on my back. He smelled of oiled wood, and during the next dance he pulled back to look at me and said I was pretty. He got me another drink.

Then we were lounging in the parking lot, his back against his beat-up Volkswagen, blowing smoke rings to the sky, watching them rise and disappear. He called me a wild grimèl[25]—although I wasn't a grimèl at all. We could still hear the crunching guitar and the keyboard. They came together to create a sometimes sultry, sometimes dreamy, and sometimes raucous feel. I wanted to listen to Michel Martelly forever, his voice loud and strong and soft and

---

24 Michel Martelly would later become President of Haiti.

25 A grimèl is a black girl with very light skin.

vulnerable. His solos were the sound of supreme confidence: not aggressive or flashy, and every impulse paid off.

The breeze made my hair go wild, as if *I* were wild, as if I could fly off and be *something*. Something like a writer. Like a doctor.

Ben and I shared stories. He wanted to join the military; I wanted to be an orthopedist.

"You're not afraid of blood?" He looked impressed. "I'd like to see you again." His grin crinkled the laugh lines around his eyes and deepened the grooves that bracketed his mouth.

My father said yes once—and the floodgates opened. My life in Thomassin became a dazzling succession of house parties, balls, gaieties, not only night after night, but also sometimes an afternoon gathering at one house followed by an evening party somewhere else. I danced, sang, and drank toasts with cheap beers. I wore trendy wide-leg jeans, white denims, belly shirts of neon colors, dresses with abstract, multicolored designs. At thirteen, I was running my own show. I understood what it meant to live at the rainbow's end and have its colors shimmer about me.

I met Ben again at another party in Pétion-Ville, in a two-story brick house with an iron balcony. Ben's eyes were chocolate-brown; his smile, easy and warm, made me feel like the only person he'd ever truly smiled at.

We were dancing by the pool when a young man bumped into Ben.

"Watch it, a-hole," Ben said with a flash of recognition in his eyes.

"What did you call me?" the other man asked.

I gave a horrible squeal, like a kitten under a rocking chair, when the stranger pushed us into the pool. Before I could take a breath, I was underwater. Wild fear grabbed the edges of my mind. Panic pounded loudly in my temples and twined my heart. I kicked and squirmed, fighting to get back to the surface. My lungs screamed for air. I was choking. I was drowning. Water went up to my nose and down into my lungs.

With one hand, Ben helped me out of the water.

In the other hand, he was holding a gun.[26]

He fired toward the sky. Gunshots popped like firecrackers. Rat-tat-tat. The air was electric—people ran around in circles and screamed, boys held

---

26 Ben was supposedly a member a FRAPH, a paramilitary group, said to be as ruthless as the Macoutes. FRAPH members received arms and training from the Haitian Armed Forces. FRAPH was accused of extrajudicial killings, forced disappearances, arbitrary arrests and detentions, rapes and other tortures and violence against women. According to Paul Farmer, thousands of civilians were killed and hundreds of thousands fled overseas or across the border into the Dominican Republic.

their girlfriends' hands. I left Ben behind and plowed through the madness to the side of the bar. I dropped to the floor, crouching beneath the porch railing. Caught in a spiral of chaos and crashing movement, charging, rushing, spinning, trampling, I couldn't see what was happening. There was more running, sauve qui peut, and dizziness. I pressed my hands against my temples as two more gunshots shattered the air.

The other guy was gone. When Ben found me in the crowd, something dangerous flickered in his eyes. He was all hard angles, like his body could cut you if you got close, if you weren't careful, if you didn't know the right way to move around him.

I knew his kind—I wouldn't be cut.

I didn't go out that much anymore because Ben materialized everywhere. Besides, there was still an embargo and the gas prices had skyrocketed, making it impossible to get around town. My father often spent half a day in a line to get his tank filled; no gas container allowed. I could still only go to school three times a week. On school days, because of the traffic caused by the long lines, the alarm clock rang at four o'clock in the morning. "C'est l'heure! C'est l'heure!" my mother chanted each morning as she opened the windows for the mountain air to rush in. We fetched water from a cistern built under the house for our bath and pressed our clothes with a smoky charcoal iron, the hollow interior filled with smoldering coals. High, spoutlike openings allowed for the coals to be fanned when swinging the iron back and forth vigorously.

Without electricity, I did my homework by candlelight. After I'd studied a chapter on the French Revolution or read about la Négritude, there was not much to do.

I didn't remember giving him my phone number. But Ben called.

We talked at night. I sat Indian-style, wringing, twirling the curly phone cord in my hand, receiver tucked between my ear and shoulder, until hours later it left my ear burning.

His voice buzzed like a bad idea.

I tried to stop talking to him—I did. But he was *there*, willing to listen, willing to understand me in ways others didn't, his availability alluring. He understood the longing to be something other than what I was, to be somewhere other than where I was. I stayed up at night, Ben on the phone, star-gazing, star-thinking, star-dreaming. Under all those stars I said the things that were most on my mind, the things I could barely stand to face when they were right there in front of me in the daylight.

I was engulfed in the incessant drone of things happening. But, with Ben, everything felt transitory, vaguely out of time. He didn't question the pure chaos in my veins, just like he didn't try to hide his trying to get into my pants. We had phone sex once, or so he thought. I was only pretending, playing Tetris silently on my Game Boy.

Maybe he was faking it too.

Ben heard my father yelling in the background. "If you ever need me to teach him a lesson," Ben said, "I'm one phone call away." His words were so sudden, so strong, their teeth marks scar me to this day.

I dreamed that night that I could no longer feel my own flesh, my hard-jutting bones, the soft places, folds and crevices. I became plenty of nothing.

I wanted to learn how to drive. Ben knew someone who knew someone else who worked at the Department of Highway Control. I got my driver's license before I ever sat behind a wheel. Papa said I was too impulsive to drive a car but, once I got the rectangular piece of colorful plastic, I knew it would be easier to convince my parents to send me to driving school.

"Teach me," I told Ben.

Mother agreed to the lessons because I told her Ben was a math teacher chez les soeurs. Truth was: Ben didn't have a job. He'd been into stealing credit card numbers on the Internet for a while. Now he admitted living off his mother's retirement money.

That afternoon, I was in the driver's seat of his red Volkswagen. He'd spent the morning at a gas station—his tank was full. Cigarette butts polluted the ashtray; the floorboards had rusted out from summers at the beach.

I'd been flirting with him out of boredom, wearing skimpy skirts and using words Mother didn't know I knew. As he showed me how to turn on the engine, how to back up, Ben was distracted by my legs. I chugged and lurched two or three times in reverse before we made it safely out of the driveway. I spun the buggy in a one-eighty. Dried grass from the summer's heat threw dust into the air, and I narrowly missed hitting a parked pickup truck. I jumped the curb, taking out several shrubs and a small tree, and regained control of the car.

We stopped the bug and walked around it. The front bumper was wrenched downward; branches weaved between it and the crammed wheel well. Ben pulled at the greenery and I joined him. With one leg propped up on the slanted bumper so he could see some more skin, I tugged on a particularly huge branch.

"I'm sorry," I said.

But I didn't mean it.

Ben said I was a fast learner, and I told him I didn't want to have driving lessons on a back road. I wanted the real thing, the treacherous Kenscoff Road leading to the mountains. This road was slim and steep, with sudden turns and a ravine on both sides, and no way to survive a fall.

I wanted someone to temper my urges to look for trouble. I expected a *No, are you crazy?* from Ben when I mentioned Kenscoff Road. That's how I usually dealt with my impulsive, crazy ideas. I stated them, and a saner person rebuffed them. Should I get a tattoo? Should I dye my hair blue? No. No. No!

But Ben said okay. So on day two, we were already on the main road. Tires spinning. Music blasting. The freedom! The excitement! I popped in a Bob Marley CD, cranked up the volume, and punched the accelerator to the floor. The car made a deep-toned hum and jolted forward with a squealing of the tires and a cloud of dust. I screamed excitedly as we sped past the huge, honking trucks.

I hit a taptap—a taxi full of people.

"Ben, you are in trouble," I said.

After all, I was thirteen. He was the adult here. He was the one who'd been willing to let me drive his car.

The other driver was surprisingly unruffled, however. One look at Ben and the stranger was flustered, nervously running his short fingers through his hair. His eyes opened wide, sending his bushy black eyebrows to the top of his forehead. He said his taptap needed serious repairs even before we'd hit it.

I hit a brand-new Honda.

The woman looked angry for a minute, and then composed herself and asked us if we'd ever heard of Amway. She said there was a reason for this to be happening, that God wanted me to become a rich girl in Haiti. As she handed me her business card, she said, "Don't worry about the repairs." So off we went, down the mountains this time.

We stopped by Estelle's house. Estelle and I had grown apart since Junior's death. The old gang had dismembered and I didn't know the kids she hung out with now. I didn't fit in. She continued to shoplift, stealing small things, tiny trophies that slipped easily into her schoolbag: earrings, bracelets, lipsticks, lollipops.

As I parked, the front of the car collapsed. Estelle's father gave Ben a hand to temporarily adjust the front of the vehicle. I let Ben take the wheel for the drive back.

We flew up the road, kissing the embankment at speeds that tested fate. Suddenly, Ben jerked the wheel and sent us flying into a cow field. The headlights bobbed into an eternity of wheat-colored grass, the moonlight miles ahead. A million voices, like flies, buzzed at the back of my neck.

And then the engine died.

I didn't expect fear to come at me so violently. I was alone with a grown man in a deserted area. He grabbed me, tried to kiss me. I wanted to say, *Oh no, you creep. Crank this puppy up and get me out of here or I'm . . . I'm . . . I'm walking!* But I simply asked him to stop. He didn't; his hands fumbled with my shirt. I could feel something in the air. Something nasty that was taking over. I had to think fast.

"I just need time," I said. "I know you're the one. I don't want to ruin it by going too fast. I've been thinking about how special this has to be."

My hands remained steady and my voice unmarked by the fear that overtook me. There was something in Ben's eyes, cold and animal—something I would not forget. He sat there, listening to the ticking of the dashboard clock, his hands locked on the wheel, his foot still on the brake pedal. The smell of burnt rubber filled the cabin.

A muscle in his cheek twitched as he drove me home. And I read his eyes. *I know where you live.*

The maid had taken a day off and Papa was busy yelling at Felix. I hung the clothes to dry, while Mother dusted and swept. Sœur peeled the potatoes over the sink, using a metal peeler with an orange plastic handle. Quartering the peeled potatoes, she placed them into a bowl of water to keep the air from turning them brown. She pulled out a metal hand-grater and grated the first quarter, careful with her strokes, watching out to keep her knuckles unscathed.

I fiddled with the knobs and the antenna of the TV until the horizontal lines disappeared and, on the TV screen, Port-au-Prince was festive. The streets had been swept clean, and crowds danced and chanted under victory arches of palm leaves and branches. A freshly painted mural depicted U.N. soldiers, their tanks and helicopters, and a smiling Aristide descending on a cloud.

The President was coming back.[27]

---

27 In October 1994, Brig. Gen. Raoul Cedras was forced into exile in Panama, along with his wife Yannick. He supposedly took up residence at "The Emperor," a building overlooking the Panama Bay in Paitilla. He is said to be writing his memoir. Cedras did give a farewell speech, but, according to the *Los Angeles Times*, the crowd drowned him out, yelling, *thief, murderer, put handcuffs on him, tie him up, zenglendo,* and so on. They hurled stones at his Jeep, forcing bodyguards to "open fire from the vehicle, sending two bursts of automatic gunfire into the humid air. Hundreds of Haitians and a few reporters dived for cover. No one was hurt."

Once we completed our chores, Sœur taught me how to make Rice Krispies Treats®. We sank to the floor cross-legged, our eyes on the TV screen. Against the wall, under the window, Papa was sleepy with his back to us. Every so often, a snore woke him; he mumbled and slept again.

seventeen

When Aristide came back and the embargo ended, the partying resumed. Somehow, I managed to avoid Ben for a few months. But then he showed up at my fourteenth birthday party, with the clear brown eyes and dimples that complemented his bright smile. He helped Estelle out of a red BMW, and she introduced him as her new boyfriend. Ben offered a strange smile, the corners of his mouth lifted, but his eyes remained dead, without the slightest twinkle in them. Finally, he showed a set of pearly white teeth and helped himself to a glass of kremas at the outdoor bar.

"Did you miss me?" he asked.

Mother pulled me aside, to a corner of the patio. "Is that Ben?" I heard suspicion in her voice. "Isn't he old for Estelle?"

"He's her new boyfriend, apparently."

"I see," she said with a dismissive gesture of her hand. "What's with the fancy car?"

I shrugged. "He's a cop now,"[28] I said.

---

28   Upon his return, Aristide dismantled the Haitian military. Members of the Haitian National Police (HNP) were soon criticized for high incidences of corruption and unwarranted violence. Several sources report that the U.S.-trained force committed serious abuses, including torture and summary executions. According to *Human Rights Watch*, the numbers in 1996 alone are horrifying. In March 1996, at least six men were killed in the slums of Cité Soleil. On August 20, 1996, two opposition politicians were murdered. On November 4, 1996, another five Haitians were shot dead. One of the men was found handcuffed while another had been shot in the head at close range. Many people were wounded in unjustifiable circumstances, and police abuse and torture of detainees increased significantly during the first seven months of 1996. In fact, eighty-six cases, in 1996 alone, were reported to the HNP's Office of the Inspector General. HNP agents beat at least five detainees to death while they were in police custody.

It was true. Ben, the center of attention that night, showed his police badge around,[29] and girls giggled, beaming in adoration. Estelle hugged him proudly, her chubby, short, and dark-skinned body and his gangly, lighter one, merging. They French-kissed in a corner.

"Look at the expensive jewelry around his neck. Smells like drug money to me."

I looked absentmindedly at the azaleas and bougainvilleas lining the side of the house. "I don't know, Maman."

I sighed and walked toward the deejay, DJ Fanfan, a handsome young man who nodded when he caught me watching him do his thing. I checked the list of songs to be played next, smiling at the familiar faces on the dance floor. The boys wore Saturday-night smiles. The girls were in dresses and slinky tops, with their hair and makeup done to perfection. I shook hands, kissed cheeks, tousled hair, and hugged. Estelle waved her arms high above her head. I gestured back, a bad feeling in the pit of my stomach. Something about Ben bugged me.

I bumped into Papa. "Do you know that guy over there?" he asked.

I looked at the boys prowling and the girls flashing a lot of skin. The loud music pounded in my eardrums. "What guy?"

"This guy who's with Estelle. Is his name Ben?"

I nodded. "It is."

"I need to talk to you."

I wanted to brush him off, but I couldn't bring myself to be disrespectful, to risk his anger at my party. I followed Papa inside his study. "What is it?" I asked.

"Do you know Ben?" he asked gravely.

"We used to be friends. He taught me how to drive."

"Oh, *that* Ben." Papa scratched his ear. "Well, apparently he's out on probation."

Mother and Matant laughed in the kitchen. They drank cocktails, dark ones, and peeped through the windows and doors to check on the "kids."

"I can't believe my little girl turned fourteen," Mother said. "It seems like only days ago when we were playing coucou, ah!"

My heart danced the cha-cha. "What was he arrested for?"

I lit up a cigarette, waited for him to ask me to throw it away.

"A drug deal gone bad," Papa said. "A fight at a pool party followed by a boy's body being found in his trunk."

A pool party? The cigarette hung loosely from my lip. I let it dangle there until the ashes fell off into a tiny gray pile on the floor.

"Damnit!" he said. "I can't believe this crooked cop is still walking around freely with his police badge."

---

29 The Haitian National Police (HNP) commenced operations in July 1995. My birthday was in April, about three months before, and yet Ben was already flashing a badge around.

The gray cigarette smoke curled up toward the discolored ceiling. I slumped down on a sofa, hoping Papa was mistaken. The adults in the kitchen moved on to talking about politics and the situation in Port-au-Prince. About the corrupt new police who'd replaced the army weeks ago.

Papa grabbed the cigarette abruptly. "Stop that."

"Are you sure about Ben?" I asked. "I mean, could just be rumors."

He threw the cigarette out the window. "Believe me, chérie, I know what I'm talking about."

I couldn't believe how calm Papa was. Was he on meds? His old self would have ended the party; he would have wielded his Uzi and threatened Ben, no matter the consequences. My heart skidded up into my throat. I needed to find Estelle. Could it be true that Ben was a murderer? I remembered the pool incident. His broody eyes, his listen-to-me lips.

I looked everywhere. Estelle and Ben were gone.

Around midnight, I dialed Estelle's phone number. No one picked up. The deejay belted out Bob Marley, the music crisp in my ears, light and airy, and I chugged my cup of cola champagne harder, only to realize how empty it was.

One in the morning. Nothing.

At two o'clock, most of the guests had left. I tried Estelle's home phone again. Nothing. As I dialed, I played connect-the-dots with the mosquito bites on my legs. Sleep crusted the corners of my eyes.

The last guests left around five a.m. I finally got Estelle's mother on the phone. She said her daughter hadn't come back, and did I have any idea where she might be?

"We need to find Estelle," I told Papa in a coarse voice after hanging up. "Maybe she's over at his house. He told me once where he lives. Would you please take me there?"

We didn't give it a second thought. Papa didn't seem to, anyway, as if his brain was on auto-pilot. We got into Papa's Trooper. The sun was just waking up, and the wind whistled through the winged windows of the car. The air whipped my hair as we passed houses patched with tin, cardboard, and plastic. Thomassin smelled of fresh leaves and donkey dung, the town so quiet at this time of day that all I could hear was the jingle bells of ice-cream carts pushed by men on their way to Pétion-Ville to sell sweet coconut popsicles. The road leading to Ben's house was narrow and crooked. My heart burned. The disturbing story about Ben haunted me.

"We are to remain calm," Papa said.

He used a rock to knock on the gate. We waited and listened; I heard the singing of psalms inside. A woman with heavy-lidded eyes and a red blouse came out of the house.

"Mwen ka ede w?" she asked. Can I help you?

"I'm sorry to bother you at this hour, ma'am, but we need to see Ben," I stammered.

She asked us to follow her, and we walked inside a room where four women prayed and incense burned with a pleasant smell. The shades were drawn. One woman in red lifted her head and nodded. Papa and I nodded back and followed her down some stairs into a basement. She knocked on a door. "Ben," she said, "there are some people here to see you."

The door opened, and the smell of marijuana rushed out along with the rank odor of alcohol and stale cigarettes. Ben emerged from the room, his lids thick, his eyes red and watery.

"Hey, Ben," I said, trying to sound casual. "How are you?"

His lips were drawn in a tight smile. His eyes were dead.

"I'm looking for Estelle," I said. "Is she here?"

He opened the door, and three other guys occupied his bedroom—all high on something. Two of them, their eyes set deep in their sockets, watched TV. The third one had passed out. He lay on a padded sofa, bathed in his own vomit, the smell of which almost made me sick. A faint lamp lit one corner of the room, and no sunlight got in. We walked in and Ben put his hand out, laying it on my arm.

"She won't come out of the bathroom," he said, and I shivered at the darkness in his voice.

His hand was raw on my skin. His expression was unreadable. How could I ever have found him cute? I noticed a gun on his desk. The air around us crackled with danger.

"You had quite a party here," Papa said with a detached voice, as if he was one of the guys. How could he sound so relaxed?

I knocked on the bathroom door. "Estelle, are you in there?"

No answer. Papa gave me a quick glance over his shoulder.

I knocked again. "Estelle, it's Jessica. Please open the door."

Ben pulled me near. His hand caressed my shoulder, slid down my back, and came to rest beneath my armpit, at the swell of my breast. "I'm sure she's okay."

My father tensed but remained quiet, probably remembering he was unarmed and outnumbered.

I heard faint crying. Oh, God! What had he done to her? Then the door cracked open, and Estelle stuck her head out. Her dark hair hung across her forehead in messy strands. She came out of the bathroom and hugged me. Her eyes were dark, hooded.

"We'll be going," Papa said.

Estelle turned away from me to look at the men. Fear whisked across her face.

Ben traced his finger along a scar on his chin. "No problem, man," he said.

He was not the man I'd met months before. His good looks were gone. He had an empty stare, a stiffness to his face. When he kissed Estelle on the lips, she didn't kiss him back. Ben's cheeks hardened and his neck tendons engorged. There was this dangerous look in his eyes again. The one I'd seen in cats' eyes while they played with their prey.

Papa, Estelle, and I made a quick exit to the car. I was about to get into the Trooper when a wave of nausea rolled over me. I dry heaved for several long moments. Fear. When the nausea abated, my temples were pounding, and the sunlight seemed too bright. I pulled myself inside the car, taking deep breaths to calm down.

On the cusp of morning, we rode into the sunrise, past the old two-story houses with porch swings and flower beds along the front walks, past the old, majestic flamboyant trees that held on to their bloody leaves.

"I was afraid they were going to hurt me," Estelle whispered. "That's why I wouldn't come out of the bathroom."

"I was afraid Ben was going to kill me," I said. "But I couldn't leave you there."

After we dropped off Estelle, Papa and I took on the quiet, bumpy Kenscoff Road, and the damp air raised goose bumps on my skin as I looked ahead into the breaking clouds, warm colors coming in to soften the sky—pinks and golds that blossomed against the horizon like jungle flowers.

But as I sucked in my breath, I couldn't taste the sunrise. I was looking over my shoulder. Because Ben knew where I lived.

eighteen

I often imagine Estelle, after she got home, the colors changing like a painter mixing pigments, swirling and clouding, the individual colors unsurpassable, yet each better than the last. It was that sort of day—a day that felt like it should belong to someone else, the way I imagine so much of her life would seem from that point on. It would be a long, long time before she'd let herself trust anyone who said they loved her.

Maybe she cried in her room, and her sister positioned a hand on her back—warm, solid. Maybe Brigitte feared Estelle would spin out of control, disappear, die—so she stayed longer than expected, her voice like a lullaby, soothing, like the blush brush that had skimmed over her face before she climbed in Ben's car.

Or maybe Brigitte had warned her against Ben, so that she grabbed Estelle's elbow and leaned in close to the girl's ear. "Why couldn't you listen?"

Maybe Brigitte believed Estelle deserved that experience, for enjoying the company of dangerous men. But what kind of people imagine for their loved ones a god who punishes the innocent and ravage women?

Maybe Estelle wrestled her arm free and stepped back. "What do you want from me?"

And her sister spun away, and away from her in her baby doll, turning and raveling the air.

I don't know what happened to Estelle that day.

I don't know what later happened to Ben.

Some said he escaped to the Dominican Republic to avoid jail time, when the uncle of the kid he was accused of murdering turned out to be close to the government. Others said he was killed in his sleep. One night, they said, his own coughing cut into his dreams. At first he thought the smoke had come from inside himself, filling up the room, leaking out the windows, blending itself into his nightmares. The family house burned down. Fire charred the lips of babies, mothers' nipples. Ben died, they said.

I never visited his neighborhood again, so I still don't know the truth about the burning. I'm not sure I remember which rue he lived on, Port-au-Prince now a maze of streets and ruelles.

"Hurt," Estelle said, "is the way we reinvent ourselves, our old skin molted and tossed."

Everything goes away eventually, I wrote. *Sins and clouds, even stars become nothing after a while.* I wrote in kamyonèt buses and taptap cabs. I talked to strangers on the way—women with budding baby bumps, men with tobacco breath. They told me about their headaches, their back pains, and swelling feet. Telling them I was not yet a doctor didn't stop them. They eyed the biology and botany textbooks I carried around.

At school, Estelle walked around in a daze, holding her notebook two-handed across her chest, the spiral wire pressing into the flesh of her hand. The sky above her looked raw, mercurochromed. She didn't answer questions. Maybe she felt her heart in her throat.

The last time we spoke on the phone, the connection was rife with static, the ghosts of other voices blurting through. Static whispered and wailed, subsided to a simmer, holding us both in its blank current. She no longer wanted to hear from me, and what did I know about her fears, about her grief?

She barely talked, in fact, until Catechism class, when Sister Claudette talked about virginity. Estelle announced she wanted to go to Hell, not Heaven. Within seconds, the voices in the classroom hushed. She said each moment of flesh had been a precious release. He'd kissed the curve at the deep of her back, turned her and kissed the taut arc of her stomach. The nun went still as a feral animal seeking camouflage.

Hearing about the sleeping pills she washed down with Diet Coke shamed me. I should have insisted on being a friend. I didn't go see her when she returned home from the hospital. Something was broken inside her, and she didn't want to see me—or anyone, for that matter. And whenever I ponder the magnitude of the job I would have had as a friend, the awesome responsibility, it seems too much, really, for the girl I was then.

nineteen

In 1995, a drunk replaced Father Aristide in the Palais National. René Préval wore t-shirts and sandals to press conferences, and the imagination of the people stained these shirts with booze. Pale and serious he was on TV, but courteous with a slow speech and far-off stare. As he smiled and glanced sideways, people held their breath, waiting for him to pass out during interviews. He didn't. Instead, he brought an atmosphere of relative peace in Port-au-Prince.

There was no legal age for drinking in 1996, so when I turned fifteen and threw another party, the thrill-craving crowd came not only for the magic of DJ Fanfan but also for the flowing alcohol. At the bar, Felix pulled jokes about the President's drinking habits all night, but I refused the offered glasses of Pinot Noir or rum-Coke. I recognized in my own drunken eyes my father's propensity for yelling and hitting. I gobbled down hors d'oeuvres—the kibbehs and akras, the tiny sausages in rolls, the spicy chiquetaille.

"Oh, mon Dieu!" Mother said in a drawl, having looked away and then back to find a plate empty. She was horrified at my appetite.

I struggled to fit in my bell-bottom jeans.

Mother chaperoned. Papa isolated himself in his room. And there was no place in the world for me but right here—at a party. I did not enjoy company, only the noise and movement of it. The music silenced the bullies who lived inside my head, the heavy percussions swallowing life's vast uncertainties. I was constantly aware of the space my body occupied. I chose my gestures and my words carefully, conscious of the dangers of spontaneity. If I let my guard down, something ugly and violent crawled out of my throat or possessed my limbs. I couldn't bring myself to love this form, this flesh; my breath squeezed through my chest like an accordion.

I was tired. Dark thoughts, the darker impulses, my fear, and my cynicism, had given me insomnia. So tired, continued existence did not seem particularly desirable. When sleep did find me, I dreamed sometimes of dying in a room cold and sterile. I saw sinister possibilities in ordinary items: kitchen knives with slight curves perfect for mincing, woven ropes—things that cannot be captured by the longing to be something other than what they are, to be somewhere other than where they are. In my veins: pure chaos.

I was too tired for conversations, about Zola's *The Human Beast* or the Machiavelli book I'd checked out from the school library. And who cared that an earthworm has five hearts or that a deer sleeps for only five minutes a day? I didn't know how to live without courting loneliness. I forgot the names of familiar babies; I didn't remember birthdays. My friends who'd moved to America during the embargo sent me cards with angels on them—Christmas angels holding trumpets, face-front in their cardboard ranks. I didn't write back. I was solitary and nothing felt real.

There was a catastrophe building inside me.

At school, I kept to myself. I read. People—including well-intentioned ones—were a nuisance. At fifteen, I thought of my own life as a novel in which we were all actors assuming roles. Equaling my existence to a plot line helped me develop a very dark sense of humor; I became observant and detached from reality. Because I distanced myself from situations, I didn't take it personally when things got ugly—that was just how the story was supposed to go. Nothing was quite real.

I sensed a kind of perversion in this way of viewing the world.

Sister Claudette caught me reading under the grapevines, skipping Math, hiding with Sartre's *La Nausée*, until Mother picked me up. Sœur was up to forty-eight books that month; she was the faster reader. I was lagging behind with forty-one; getting in trouble with Administration was a chance I was willing to take.

Sister Claudette didn't punish me. She liked me; she believed I had a good heart. Somehow our conversation led to faith and service, and Sister Claudette said that love was a decision. "If you wait until you feel love for others, you'll never love anyone. You need to take the decision to love them, and then stick to that decision."

She got into a very deep thought, and I wondered about the life she'd left behind in Paris to become a teacher in Port-au-Prince, and later an administrator. I wondered if she was varicosed under her habit.

I was finishing *The Orient Express*, rushing through the last pages so I could start *Why Didn't They Ask Evans?* when the girl stood in front of me, two sidekicks in her shadow.

"Hey, you," she said, towering over me. "Tell me something." She had a mean, scrunched-up face, twitching like a rat's. She fumbled in the pocket of her school uniform. She finally retrieved a small mirror and put it to my face. "How can you bear to look at yourself?" she asked. "You're *so* damn ugly." She sneered.

It was May, almost June, the air fragrant with jasmine. Ylang-ylang blossoms burst like stars in the trees; their delicate custard scent infused the heated air. I registered the hurtful impact that the words were supposed to have, but they didn't slash their way through me. My emotions were delayed: Pain, joy, anger—they usually took their sweet time, which allowed me to look unimpressed. I was trying to make sense of the conversation, trying to reacquaint myself with the real world. I couldn't understand why this girl was even talking to me. I spent so much time reading that I often found myself stuttering when other students addressed me, as if my mouth had grown rusty.

"What do... do you want?" I asked, my jaw in need of a tune-up. "Who... who are you?"

She mocked me. "Who... who are you?"

I finally recognized her. She'd read some of her original poems at the Concours d'Art Oratoire, the school literary contest. I'd won first place and landed a set of three Agatha Christie books (translated in French, *S'il Vous Plaît!*) along with a framed certificate signed by Sister Claudette. Soraya was being a sore loser.

I'd seen Soraya around the school before. Between chapters, I often people-watched, observing students leaving for home in the afternoon, vendors of ice-cream and Oreo-like cookies in their colorful straw hats, unschooled Haitian teenagers-turned-street-pharmacists who held up buckets filled to the rim with long-expired prescription drugs. Soraya's mother picked her up in a beige Nissan; she wore humongous dark glasses. One day, the mother took these glasses off to powder her face in the rearview mirror, and that's when I saw it: the horrible black eye.

Another day, Soraya's father was riding shotgun, and the couple was still arguing when the mother parked the car. The windows were up, but I could see their angry faces, could imagine their angry words. I don't think anyone else saw it—the way he grabbed her wrist. The firm set of his brow, the rigidity of his mouth, reminded me of my own father.

I wanted to feel sorry for Soraya, but she was a bully. Anger caught along the base of my neck like needles, but it still wouldn't show on my face—it lingered inside, acidic, caustic, fuming. I was angry at her, at her violent father, at my own father.

I gently pushed away from my face the hand shoving the mirror. "I hope Daddy doesn't break that mirror in your face and make you as ugly as I am," I said. "When he's done rearranging your mother's face, I mean. Something tells me you might be next."

She held her breath. For a moment, I thought she was going to hit me. I was taken aback by my own conviction and ferocity. I didn't think I still had that much mean in me, the hot bad words suddenly crowding my throat. My pulse twitched, and yet I could tell my facial expression remained courteous, almost kind. I went back to reading. So many books to explore, so little time. Reading: a compulsion. Following Agatha Christie's novels, *La Bête Humaine*, *L'Étranger*, and *La Porte Étroite* were on my list.

After the bell rang, I saw Soraya on my way to algebra class. Her eyes were red and she was sniffling. I was still gripped by the raw, naked feeling, the acute bewilderment that had come with the realization of my unfocused anger and the indifference I felt toward her pain.

No one deserved the words I'd told her.

This is the first day I ever remember feeling lonely. Before that, yes, I sensed I was a bit weird—a loner. But I was okay with it. I used to think that I didn't belong because I didn't choose to. After I talked to Soraya, I realized that I'd never belong even if I tried to.

I felt doomed.

It was summer when I tried to kill myself—something about the long, airless days in Thomassin, the little waves of heat that shivered on top of the cars. I went to Mother's dresser and eyed her bottle of sleeping pills.

At first, I was afraid to make a move, despite this human ache, the worry. I looked up and studied the heaviness around my eyes.

When I swallowed the pills, they stuck in my throat and worked my gag reflex. I spit them out into the bathroom sink, picked them back up, wet and slimy, and swallowed them again. Soaked in sweat, I went back to my room and waited for transformation, for ascension out of this world. I clasped my hands over my mouth to quiet my rasping breath. My heart beat in wildly syncopated rhythms.

But death did not come.

I ate a box of Danish cookies in the dark. My mouth was open as I chewed—a loud mastication, like tchaka corns crushed in a mortar and pestle. It was the only sound. I could feel my epiglottis shift when I swallowed. Then I stood at the window and watched the different degrees of darkness, the branches of trees obscuring the stars. I held on to the gauzy curtain, feeling the grittiness between my fingers, my head and shoulders dangerously close to floating. How spiritual the streets were in their absolute stillness and silence.

I went back to bed in the too-quiet silence that made me believe that I could hear my every breath and heartbeat.

After I was dead, I woke up with my belly on fire and vomit hot in my mouth. Another burst resurged, trickling upwards, anti-gravity. My fingertips tingled, my eyes burned.

I puked on the sheets, all over the floor. Then my empty stomach turned over, sending a slice of pain through my midsection.

I was very much alive.

By dawn I had thrown up everything there was to throw up into the toilet, shuddering on the bathroom tile, the blade of the oscillating fan in the attached bedroom nick-nick-nicking at its metal cage.

Hollowed out and underwhelmed, I cleaned up after myself.

Mother came into my room, looking for her bottle of pills, which contained Flanax, I learned, a pain reliever. Not Valium, as it read on the label. If there had been any disappointment in that moment, it was too fleeting to be measured or acknowledged.

twenty

I couldn't stop eating. I felt a hole inside me—it was not *like* a hole, but a physical vacuum. I wanted *something* to lead me to militance, to strength, or at least solace; food temporarily drove me to oblivion. I focused on eating and let myself go; Mother called my matted hair a rat's nest, and sometimes took a comb to it. I spread orange marmalade on toasted French baguettes—thick and warm and buttery. The knife came and went across the plate. I drank over-sweetened passion fruit juice and glasses of powdered milk with Milo. In front of Sainte Rose de Lima, gummy rats and Marie cookies called to me.

I got toothaches, which I endured—I thought about feet that stepped on beds of coals in mystical ceremonies. I fell asleep in class and dreamed of reaching into swirling water to save something, someone. The force of the water dissolved my flesh and left my bones polished, white.

I hid peanut butter and cheese sandwiches inside my desk, took mouthfuls as Monsieur Augustin scribbled equations on the board. I used a spoon to eat peanut butter out of the jar, until the metal scraped against the glass bottom. At recess, I bought Spam sandwiches from Madame Vitiello's snack bar, thick prune pies and ice-cold bottles of Cola Champagne. I saved four or five croissants in a brown paper bag for an afternoon snack.

Faces surrounded me, and yet I felt lonely. Students in white blouses and shiny shoes wore bright smiles. Their faces, freckled, smirking, running past—a blur. Arms locked to each other like jewelry clasps, they roamed in pack and whispered about boys and makeup.

After school, I took an extra-curricular cooking class and learned how to fold intricate hors d'oeuvres while I stared outside the window at the clock vine sprawling along a fence. When Mother picked me up, the taste of *batonnets au fromage* was still on my tongue. I begged her for Eskimo ice cream bars on our way home.

One day, Mother was late. I sat in the school chapel, by the sunken, slightly hunched Christmas tree, when the landscapers behind the window began to sing, picking up the tune from one another, their song rhythmic and hypnotic, like a mantra. It spoke of death and suffering and God.

Someone would listen. I found Father Israel.

Father Israel didn't hide behind a wooden confessional; he sat on a sofa at his private home, blocks away from my own house. Next to a kneeler, he listened. When I digressed, citing passages of an Agatha Christie murder mystery, I could tell he was confused.

"Are you trying to tell me you might hurt someone?" he asked.

No. I simply loved books—new ones for their freshness, used ones for their mystery. I took them to the waterfall in Thomassin or up on the roof of the house my parents had built. At night, I read late under the bedcovers with a flashlight. I loved words. They tingled my bones. They made me feel part of something greater than myself. I'd become one of those people who scribbled on napkins at the table and on the back of grocery store receipts, eager to create a new world and pour my entire imagination into it. I used words to unravel the knots that were tied long ago.

Father Israel didn't question my visits. He didn't rush me. A cigar burned in the ashtray and the maid, Rosita, made chicken stew or seasoned goat meat in the kitchen. I was grateful to God because I'd survived my desperate suicide attempt, and glad that I could walk through the front doors of Father Israel's house, see him watching the news in the living room, hear Rosita say she'd saved me a plate of food in the refrigerator and all it needed was a few minutes in the stove.

I told Father Israel about *Becoming Abby,* a book by some obscure writer whose name I still can't remember. I wanted to be wild, surrender my Catholic chains, break a few hearts. Bad girls didn't feel sadness or loneliness. Not Abby, anyway. She was funny, unrestrained. She was *liberated.* Unlike me—so plain, so unimpressive. I wanted to be the kind of girl who'd steal smokes from her mother's purse and booze from her father's cabinet, who'd sneak into R-rated movies at the local theater and lose her virginity to a boy who had his own car and liked to "do it" in the backseat, become a dangerous girl who'd drive in the middle of the road and wouldn't obey stop signs. I imagined that girl, hurried, naked—sweating with a forbidden lover on her twin-sized bed, under striped sheets and posters of boy bands, feeling no regret when daylight came, turning the sky from purple to blue, and then to a shocking bright light. But I barely understood the language of flirting, dating, love, passion. While Papa broke the porcelain vases, and Mother went to bed with a crust of tears drying on her cheeks, I stared at the dark television, and in the curve of the screen, my reflection was at the end of a long, black hallway.

I told Father Israel about the pills. "I want to stop feeling so much," I said.

He listened. He let me get it out. He didn't offer advice. In the garden, lizards lurked, waiting, tongue-quick, for flies.

Father Israel's eyes burned with a kind of fascination; he wanted to save me. He believed in God too much. He didn't understand that Jesus sometimes took extended vacations, long enough to allow my father to get in a rage and throw my mother against a wall, leaving me with tears stinging behind my eyelids and a hard painful lump in the back of my throat.

I fell asleep before the act of contrition. I hadn't slept for days.

When I woke up, it was still light out and the birds were singing fall. I found Father Israel in the backyard. He absolved me under the orange tree.

I saw myself the way Father Israel might see me—my full breasts, my curvy limbs. He caught my eyes as they scanned his broad body, as I imagined holding him, swimming out to meet the curving, lolling wave of his embrace. I smiled because the thought was a surprise. It was so unlike me—nouveau and liberating. It offered possibilities, twists, thrill. I'd never considered something so forbidden before.

Maybe there was hope.

Maybe Abby one day might come out. I was human, after all—mutable. Nothing in the world was ever otherwise.

Father Israel fidgeted under the stare; he cleared his throat.

"I'm listening, *Jessica*," he said. He stressed my name, sounding it out like a foreign word unpleasant on the tongue.

I stood up and cleaned my bell-bottom jeans of grass and mud.

I thanked him and walked home, thinking about the next party, the next slow dance I would care to accept. Maybe I would let a boy get close. Maybe I wouldn't talk about Voltaire or Sartre or Shakespeare. The New Kids on the Block were no longer in vogue. When I got home, I put up a poster of that new singer I heard about. He sang, "*What a piece of body, girl, tell me where you get it from.*"

Buju Banton. Yeah, that was his name. Buju Banton.

twenty-one

At sixteen, it was mad love, filled with giggles and stomach-churning excitement.

He wore a knitted Jamaican tam, and something about the way his face animated filled my body with bones again. Pierre filled the void of loneliness that had been inflating inside me. He filled it with something dense and heavy like liquefied gold.

Pierre was a mystery that embodied all my new curiosity about the opposite sex.

On Fridays, we ate at Pizza du Village, in Thomassin, where there were round, marble-topped tables and wrought-iron chairs. The restaurant smelled of disinfectant and clean tablecloths. Before the waiter, a skinny man with a high, glossy forehead, refilled my glass of lemonade, mouth bulging, I opened up about Papa and his episodes, about my parents' arguments at dinner, their silence in the car, the drama that never ceased, the crises that rose out of nowhere. And I told him I was a virgin.

"It makes me feel ugly," I said. "The fights, I mean."

The waiter brought us slices of mango, and we enjoyed the slippery texture of the fruit, that mix of sweet and tang.

"You're beautiful," Pierre said.

I pointed at the empty bowl of mango. "You ate it all."

He laughed, and I liked the rich, full-throated sound of his laughter. He pointed at my plate. "You ate the pizza."

I had eaten the *whole extra-large, thick-crusted thing.* I felt physically ridiculous, like my body was the punch line to a bad joke. We changed the subject sharply, the way people avoid potholes on a muddy street. Girls in my class had had sex and others talked endlessly about it, their tongues swollen from gossip. When I told Pierre that I wanted him to be my first, I brought a wave of red to his face. My words were sudden, like a sneeze, a brain freeze, an itchy spot on the skin.

When he kissed me, I could taste mangoes on his mouth. My body hummed inside itself. Through the fabric of his t-shirt, I could feel his rib cage tremble from internal percussion.

His voice was made of soft sounds, like a river unfurling: "I'm beginning to like you."

He hung tacky souvenirs off the rearview mirror in his Jeep. He clean-shaved his head (*tèt kale bobis*) for his cap to fit better. He stared at my mouth when he wanted to kiss me. He bought me silly presents like a silver whistle and Flintstones vitamins. He liked to hold hands, and he liked to watch X-rated movies, and he liked to fix Papa's computer. He wore a strand of my hair around his neck; he'd cut the hair himself. From my own neck hung a human tooth. It was his tooth, which he gave me in a box for Valentine's Day.

He said, "You have great tits."

I paid attention during Biology, as I still wanted to become a doctor. And during Literature and French. The rest of the time, I thought about Pierre in his faded jeans and boots. I loved him more than a person ought to love one thing and, in our conversations, the words *sex* loomed just around the corner.

On Fridays, he picked me up from Sainte Rose de Lima in his Jeep with no air conditioning in the Port-au-Prince heat. It had a faulty exhaust so we couldn't breathe too deeply while we cruised. When Pierre allowed me to drive, traffic slowed, car horns erupted, and motorbikes wormed their way around us. He reminded me to engage the blinkers and adjust the mirrors. His eyebrows were bunched at the center of his forehead. I wanted to smooth them back out, one over each eye.

Two roads converged at a yellow light and, as the signal autumned into red, a kamyonèt full of people and chickens stalled in the middle of Rue Faubert. On the radio, they said a journalist has been killed. In the background of the news report, a woman was crying. The music and rhythm of her wailing would stay with me, a voice that carried more than its weight.

Pierre fed me. He stopped at Pâtisserie Marie Béliard and, fascinated, watched me eat the harlequins au chocolat in the Jeep. When I offered him something from the white carton box, he patted his abdomen. "I'm all right." He touched my hand like it was a kitten in need of reassurance.

"Did you know?" he asked. "It takes a year for a body to purge itself down to bone."

He stroked my knee, his thumb moving in circles. As I pressed my hand over his, I thought about resurrection—the dead back in their skins and forgetting to rejoice.

He said, "You're beautiful." His lips tasted of sugar cane and lemon juice.

We were alone in the house that afternoon. A layer of dust settled on us in my father's study, a space that haphazardly stored belongings and relics of questionable necessity, all spilling from cardboard boxes labeled for contents they no longer held. The shelves were jammed with books; the musty smell of paper and ink, bindings and glue surrounded us.

His hands traced my neck, my earlobes, the inside of my forearms. I explored the rasp of his tongue, the sharpness of his teeth. I heard the metallic rasp of his zipper, and his heart beat a tide against my chest.

I wanted him to take away my hunger.

Pierre fumbled with the condom wrapper, tore it with his teeth. I played the banjo on his naked thighs, his magnificent calves, his dimpled knees, every particle alive in the filtered sunshine of the room.

"Am I hurting you?" he asked.

I had no voice, so I shook my head *no*. His weight against me was comforting. My soul had left my body for years and was just now coming back.

"Why are you crying?" he asked after it was over.

My throat was tight. "I'm hungry."

There is a kind of hunger that feeds on life.

We spent days naked—unashamed of our imperfections. While my parents completed their eight-to-five days, and Sœur took summer classes at the Faculté des Sciences, we made good use of the living room sofa, the kitchen counter, the stairwell. I told him what I wanted (*There. No, a little bit more to the right. Yes, there.*). My skin felt striped with heat where we touched. We learned the best ways to a climax-inducing cunnilingus, tried flavored condoms, went on a quest to find the g-spot. He drew sketches of me on construction paper, just like in *Titanic*.

We fed on Spam sandwiches and chocolate mousse. While he put rollers in my hair in front of Mother's vanity mirror, he talked about reincarnation, and how certain souls were meant to find each other in different lives. He believed with absolute candor that we already knew each other in a past realm, and everything revolved around this conviction.

Pierre introduced me to his parents, told them I was the girl he would marry some day. He'd taken off his Jamaican tam at the table. He weighed only

130 pounds. I could see his collarbone, and once spent two hours carrying him on my back at a school fair.

His father frowned. "Don't be ridiculous. You're a kid." His lips were thick and petulant.

I focused on the lasagna.

His mother talked to me in a soft, gentle tone all through dinner, her eyebrows pitched knowingly, thin and steep as the stiletto heels on the shoes she'd kicked off. The cat sat back on her haunches to sharpen her claws on Pierre's jacket, slung over the back of a chair in the dining room. Outside the window, the fading sun smudged the treetops with gold. Mangoes were everywhere—the slender, flat leaves, branch tips thick with fruit. That night, Pierre slid a love note into my palm. *If you were to ever leave me, I would kill you.* The wind rose and swept white petals from the trees in his parents' side lawn.

When his father took away the Jeep, Pierre took on a journey toward beatitude. At six o'clock in the morning, he walked to the crowded bus station on Route Nationale Numéro Un. The kamyonèt he boarded there traveled to the ghetto of Delmas 2 and the outstretched hands of children in rags. The next bus climbed up to the city of Pétion-Ville, and the last one up the mountains of Thomassin. When he showed up drenched in sweat, a backpack on his shoulders, Pierre kissed me as though he'd been drowning without my presence. He didn't complain about the two-hour commute. He made me feel beautiful and lush, and in the evening he returned home with the heat of my breasts cupped in his hands.

He defied his father when his family decided that we spent too much time together—the uncles and aunts serving as the unsympathetic jury. He called me, his voice dull and weary until his breathing became the only evidence that he was still there, waiting for me to say something—anything—so we could go on talking, filling up the minutes after every fight with his father. I imagined him on his bed on those afternoons, like a corpse waiting for the soul's flight. The sun pulled the sky into its heat, scorched it bare of clouds, of birds.

twenty-two

At the start of the new school year, Pierre got the Jeep back from his father. Sometimes he picked me up early from school, his smile devilish, his enthusiasm contagious. He told jokes at which his own lusty laughter sounded in the hot air before mine did. He talked in a frantic stream of words that verged on hysteria and kept me tense and pleasurably horrified. I was used to him, but constantly fascinated, like a magician's nervous rabbit. I liked his irreverent nature. I carried a snapshot of him the way good Catholic girls carried mass cards of their name saints.

I ditched algebra class to attend the funeral of a man I did not know with Pierre. We did things like that, he and I—we pretended to be invisible and people-watched. I'd changed into a black suit jacket with matching casual pants, and the harsh fabric rubbed painfully against my thighs.

He said, "I have to believe there is something behind this miraculous world."

"I've applied to med school," I said in the car. "Notre-Dame. I'm going to be a doctor."

He smiled. "I can see it."

"I don't know," I said. "Sometimes I worry about not finding the time to write. What about you? Have you checked out the computer science programs?"

"Not yet," he said. "Tell me a story."

I told him about Pipo, my childhood dog, under the bed; I thought he was just sleeping. Then I rose from a bad dream, shocked by the cold floor into waking, and there he was—heartbeat missing, limbs stiffening. Outside the bedroom window, I could hear insects hoarsely singing, bowing ugly violins. There's a pain in the world that follows people like their shadow, despite reason and proportion. But stories, even sad ones, keep the darkness from wrapping us in its long, barbed sleeves. They spin us out and back into their embrace. We glide in their magic, beaming, breathless—forgetting what worries we have.

In algebra class, I had pencils and a desk that opened from the top. Sines, cosines, and tangents. Then a lecture about the dangers of unruly behavior. During Catechism, slumped over the table, I dreamed of Pierre's lips, of a glass of Barbancourt Rum, of a cigarillo's fragile column of ash. Jesus: remote and unknowable, my sins clinging to me like vines. And then there was food. I wanted to stop eating. But I got fidgety around food. I was not gaining any weight, but my dentist worried. I placidly opened my mouth, allowing Dr. Dougé to gaze into the blackness.

He brought me fresh mangoes from La Plaine—as round as shoulders. Bob Marley was blaring from the speakers. He was oozing with nerves, his skin stretched over his cheekbones.

Bruises peppered his arms and back.

"My father found out about my grades," he said. "He's blaming you."

On Thomassin Road, he cranked up the volume, and punched the accelerator to the floor. The car made a deep-toned hum and jolted forward with a squealing of the tires and a cloud of dust. "Let's drive off a cliff," he said. "Let's end it all." The car was strong with the smell of cigarette smoke and stale beer.

"Stop! I don't want to do this!" I slapped wildly at him and he shrunk from my flailing hands.

He pumped the brakes and avoided the cliff.

He was barefoot, and his toes were playing with the slim leg of the kitchen table. I was melting butter in hot milk. I'd learned the bread pudding recipe in my cooking class at Sainte Rose de Lima, and according to Madame Gousse, this recipe was copied, loaned out, scribbled on note cards for generations in her family, passed on by grandmothers and great-aunts. From Madame Gousse, I'd also learned to bake a *Bûche de Noël* with three layers of chocolate genoise, brushed with kirsch-flavored sugar syrup. But nothing beat the soothing calm of kneading bread for homemade *pudding de pain,* of combining the sugar, eggs, cinnamon, nutmeg, and vanilla.

Pierre got butter from the Frigidaire, brought me the electric mixer, and we added the milky mixture. On the TV screen, there was a horse skeleton in the bristly weeds somewhere, the skull facing the desert.

"Tell me a story," Pierre said. His eyes were sharp and darting. His fight with his father had pressed something grave into his face.

I poured some rum in the mix of bread, eggs and butter. "I want you to cut my hair."

I placed the bread in a lightly greased casserole and sprinkled with raisins.

He poured the batter on top of the bread. "What?" And I noticed once again how handsome he was, in an uncomplicated way.

I turned the knob to 350 degrees, then handed him the scissors. "Here." We were surrounded with open bags of *Chico* cheese curls and newspapers sticky with *titos* candy. "I have to get rid of something," I said. "Take it away."

My hair reached my shoulders—thick, unmanageable. I told him about a man in Christ-Roi. His garden was overgrown with roses, bougainvillea, and there was a muck of vines. White hair and a grizzled white beard framed Papi's plump, rosy cheeks, until one day he quit his Santa Claus look. With his shaved head, he had a cherubic face usually seen in newspaper portraits of serial rapists. His long neck held his head in a dangerous balance high up over his shoulders, like a marionette's. There was something different about his personality, too. One day, he enveloped my head with his palms and twisted it upwards; he put his mouth over mine, leaving a thick layer of warm saliva. I couldn't decide whether he'd become a crazy person acting sane or if he was still a sane person acting crazy.

Hair can change you. Think about Samson.

His hand was unsteady as he attempted to cut the first lock. "I can't do it." He looked tired and old and worn, and there were small twin lines between his heavy brows.

I impressed a stern, moist kiss on his hairless cheek, and then grabbed the scissors. "Like this."

"Oh, mon Dieu!" he whispered as the hair fell on my neck, on my shoulders.

I took the lock—it was soft and soothed my hand, my skin. I wondered if hairdressers ever got distracted, just stroked and stroked until the person in the chair became alarmed.

"There's no turning back." I closed my eyes and flinched.

Lock after lock, he cut. My hair smelled of flowers that had dried—in my mind, I named the flowers. His fingers played the piano on my cropped scalp. He needed a haircut too. Thick brown locks curled over the tips of his ears. He laid his head against my thigh. We had trouble staying close without touching.

Something was wrong. And it wasn't just about his father. I could see it now. My pulse tripped and stumbled.

"What is it?" I asked.

He forced the words out. "I'm leaving."

Questions crowded my thoughts. I didn't know where to begin. My throat hurt when I swallowed.

His gaze was slow. "My father is sending me to Miami." He sank to the ground, rested his head on my knees, put it away. "He wants to take me away from you."

My eyes burned. "It would have happened sooner or later anyway," I said, "the sliding apart of us two."

"Don't say this, Jess."

"Love doesn't last." My mouth felt uncoordinated. "Love destroys you. It crawls into your lap and wrecks you from the inside out."

It would have been easier to believe this.

Later, my father was angry about the haircut. In ancient times, he said, Israelites shaved the heads of their unfaithful wives. I could tell by his voice that he had a cold, the sound trapped in his nose.

"Want some bread pudding?" I asked.

A muscle twitched in his left cheek.

The day Pierre left, the sky was a sharp Sunday blue—and yet remote, cold, distant. Grief flickered in his eyes, but he blinked them away. In the front yard of the house in La Plaine, I knew I should reach out for him, knew I should hold him so tight against me that we would melt into our sorrow together, but the thought of physical contact overwhelmed me. Things screamed inside me and my eyes felt hot.

We promised to stay in touch. We promised to see each other soon—against all odds.

The corner of my mouth twitched.

"Tell me this will work," Pierre said.

A knot blossomed in my throat where the word *yes* should be. His eyes welled up. He clamped his lips, as if he could trap his sadness inside.

"Move along now," his father said, guiding Pierre toward the Jeep. "Keep it moving."

And the mellow voice made it sound reasonable.

So Pierre climbed in his father's 4x4—erect, already a ghostly figure, a stranger in the making.

twenty-three

The roosters crowed at four as the yellow dawn appeared, and again at seven, after the sun, bright and cheerful, had completely risen above the rim of the earth. Crisp and cold mountain air filtered through the windows of my bedroom, carrying the smell of pine trees, and that, more distant, of Haitian coffee and biswit, soft bread toasting in the oven.

It was 1999. I was 18, a med student at Notre-Dame University, in Port-au-Prince. I was in love with the *idea* of being a doctor. I imagined limbs stretched across the cold steel of an operating table. I would open people's insides: see parts of them they'd never seen, parts of themselves they could only imagine. I would fix them, and then, with delicate stitch work, I would seal them back up.

For a while, Pierre's ten-page handwritten letters trickled in, and I traced with my fingertips the loops and swirls of his *t*'s, *l*'s, and *o*'s. I sat on the balcony to read his words and my eyes, I imagined, glittered with secrets beneath a gold and languid sky. Once a month, he sent me ninety-minute Sony audiotapes with his voice recorded on both sides of the cassettes. When the Internet grew, we switched to emails and instant messages on ICQ and MSN. Even in the distance, we were merged.

But it was crazy to put so much into something so fragile.

He was not coming back.

When the letters stopped, it burned me with weeping.

I found my parents at the breakfast table, Mother in a pink, oversized nightgown, having coffee, Papa wearing an old Rhum Barbancourt t-shirt, beige shorts and leather sandals, cutting an avocado in pieces to accompany the ground corn, his knife knocking against his plate.

My parents spent their days listening to the news on the radio. The government lied about the weather. Lied about the sun, moon, stars. The country contracted, expanded, broke apart. I needed a new paradise.

"What about breakfast?" Mother asked when I grabbed the car key.

The wind brought the giggles of children playing on the hills, the big laugh of our maid Marie, and the sound of her vigorous hands scrubbing clothes in the basin. Birds chirped in the pure blue sky. I looked out, at the soybeans, lush and green, at the corn, as high as my waist.

"I'm running late for Chemistry."

In the street, I drove past the burned church, the orphanage, and the ruins of the old cemetery. I overtook several huge trucks carrying gravel or water, and the air against my face was clean and fresh. The floorboard holes of my third-hand Isuzu Trooper were open windows on the road beneath my feet, and the back seat windows slid down as if cranked by invisible ghosts.

In Pétion-Ville, radios of street vendors blared news reports. I took new routes across town and found myself driving down unfamiliar streets, which gave me the most exhilarating feeling: the realization that not a single person on earth knew where I was.

I was not lost, just temporarily misplaced.

I made a right turn and I was back in the familiar crawl of traffic, horns cursing red lights. I crossed Rue Ogé, saying its name aloud like a good friend's name, although it was a street where nothing occurred that had touched anyone I knew. I drove down Delmas and turned into Musseau, a long, narrow, and sun-baked street, and drove among faded yellow and rose houses, battered dogs, and laundry swaying on lines. Old men sat under the bougainvilleas with their pipes.

I found Seb and Dave in the yard. They were the new college dropouts I hung out with since I found it unbearable to sit still in class.

Dave lay on a bench surrounded by breadfruit trees. "What about school?"

"Can wait. I was hoping to find a quiet place to write."

"But we're going to the movies!" Seb said.

He leaned against the hood of his race car, eyes red, reeking of alcohol, and Dave sat on the gravel floor, laughing at him. "You're drunk."

Dave said he'd drive. His teeth sparkled like pearls, and his beautiful eyes also seemed to grin. Around the corner, he stopped the Trooper to buy some pistachios from Philomène. The street vendor had deep, brown eyes, just like my grandmother Simone. And she had dimples—if you ever caught her smiling.

The traffic on Delmas was outrageous.

"Dave thinks you're unhappy," Seb said.

"I'm not unhappy."

"You live your life in your head," Dave said.

We reached the Imperial Theater and I got the tickets and popcorn. The lady at the booth told us the movie might get canceled; employees were caught in traffic downtown because of some protest. I ordered a Prestige at the food stand, but Dave took away my cigarette.

"Bad for your health. You should know—you're going to be a doctor."

The movie was canceled and we got a refund for the tickets, ate the popcorn in the car, and ended up at Munchies, a busy restaurant in Pétion-Ville. I paid for the beers, pizzas, and cheese sticks, and got a pack of Comme Il Faut cigarettes. The waiter had a bristly face, disheveled hair and dark-circled eyes.

I didn't eat. The thought of eating and drinking was repulsive. Dave and Seb gorged their stomachs full, and I felt hunger for their hunger, for their appetites, swiftly satisfied. I leaned on the handrail of the balcony. The alcohol was bitter and went well with the inner pain. One long drag of a Comme Il Faut and I relaxed.

Dave hugged me. "Wanna go?"

He had an oval face, curly brown hair, and large and luminous eyes. He kissed me and his lips were cool; it felt good to be against his warm shirt. But only for a minute. I didn't want a relationship. I imagined Pierre in Miami. How, no matter how flat and tough he held his mouth, his eyes sparkled. He couldn't help it.

Sometimes I forgot he'd been gone for a year and waited for him to appear at the front door.

We went back to the car, the day now grainy and muggy and musty.

The crowd in front of Seb's house forced Dave to slow down. I had seen the mob in action before; I was still not ready for this.

We came upon a body on the pavement, and a man asked us to stop the car. Dave knew the man. "What's going on?"

"She was hit by a police car. Hit and run."

The woman lay there, like a broken doll, limp with one arm pinned beneath her at an awkward angle. So much blood. Despite the blood, despite the jagged lacerations and discolored contusions, Dave knew this face. It was a face he'd seen every day—how could he not know it?

"Philomène," he said, and it was not a question, and his legs buckled under him.

It was the street vendor from earlier. She seemed little more than a mangled lump in a spreading puddle of blood, curled up on her side, pistachios scattered around her. A worn sneaker lay several feet to the side.

"Do something," Seb told me.

I was not a doctor yet. What did he expect?

I got out of the car and, as I crouched down next to Philomène, her eyes rolled. She went limp, her pulse weak and irregular, a slight gasp at the end of each breath.

"We need to bring her to the hospital," Dave said. "She's losing consciousness."

But she'd lost so much blood already. As they put her in the trunk of the Isuzu Trooper, I knew it was already too late. "Don't move," I told her in my head. "It'll be over soon. It will be calm again. And you will be free. Your worries will go. You'll feel the kind of peace you never have felt in Haiti. You want that, don't you? You do. I know you do."

Philomène's body was cold when I touched her hands, and the tracery of red blood vessels in her cheeks drained of color. As her body settled gradually into the rigor of death, heartbeat missing, limbs stiffening, her face assumed a strangely gentle, slightly mischievous smile. A pressure built in my head and face. I could not be a doctor. I knew, right then, that I would drop out of medical school.

twenty-four

Mother was on the balcony, where the strung-up laundry lines sagged like shortened smiles, where the acacia had tossed its pollen. Wearing shorts and a halter-type blouse with embroidery and pretty buttons, she stared in adoration at a spineless climbing cactus—a gift from my father. She was here every night, and I'd taken the habit of following her outside.

"What is it called?" I asked.

"Reina de la noche. Princess of the night. Its flower blooms only in the night and only once a year."

"Have you ever seen it?"

"Once."

Mother sighed—she brought her hand to her forehead and squeezed her temples, closing her eyes. The flowers were not in bloom tonight. She described the exuberance of white, the amplitude of flesh and volupté. When that one night came, the princess splurged, she didn't hold back, she spent it all.

"The first time your father saw a reina, he was hanging from a tree, wearing his mother's high-heeled shoes. He was only a boy."

Mother didn't know she was telling stories; she was simply talking, and what she said had a beginning, middle, and end. She told me about my father's mother, Man Simone, the school teacher. My father was an adventurous ten year-old boy, running wild around the neighborhood, creating mischief. Man Simone locked his clothes and shoes in a cabinet to coerce the young boy into staying home.

"Your father couldn't be detained. He put on his brother's Sunday best and his mother's high heels."

I'd heard this story before. In the 1950s, bordering the Boulevard de La Liberté in Saint Marc, were low, small houses, all alike with a large porch in the front, and a small backyard—so close one to another that everyone knew what was going on at the neighbor's. No phones. No electricity. Terra cotta pitchers kept drinking water cool. Boulevard de la Liberté led west to L'Ecole des Frères de l'Instructon Chrétienne, the Catholic school Papa attended, and east to Pivert Street and the pastry shops of Man Dodo and Madame Zius, known for their delicious bonbon siwo.

Mother was not theatrical when telling her stories because she was good at it.

"Before noon," she said, "the entire neighborhood was talking about it—your father walking around in women's shoes. Your grandmother came running after him with a martinette. Goule climbed an avocado tree and hung from a branch, threatening to let go."

It wasn't unusual for Man Simone to whip my father with a belt or a yardstick or a branch stripped from a sassafras or persimmon sapling.

Hanging from the avocado tree, my father saw the plant; the flowers were not in bloom in the middle of the day, but there was still something mesmerizing about the way the princess climbed the wall of Madame Zius' shop.

I followed Mother back inside for another sleepless night of writing. I, too, was a reina de la noche, a creature of the night—only after dark did I enter the province of words, a domain without clocks or despair. I thought of the unpredictable beauty that sometimes emerged from my father, smoothing away his frown, crinkling his lips into a smile.

The Reina de la noche is called a Cereus plant. It was growing rapidly and buds appeared, attempting to bloom, but sugar ants attacked the vulnerable buds. Mother sprayed the princess with plant soaps and oils.

Mother didn't know my father until he was in his twenties, but she knew the numerous stories of his childhood. Papa, dark and brooding, seldom talked to me about his past, about Saint Marc, so I got the stories second hand. I was mesmerized by the Boulevard de La Liberté, where children walked around with straw baskets to collect sapotiy, pomegranates, cherries, grapes, quenêpes, mangoes, and oranges from their neighbors' trees, following the paths that snaked around the seasonal, tropical spinach plants, and the breadfruit trees. Papa climbed the coconut and almond trees, scaring away the birds that sallied for insects around the bends—the white-winged warblers and the tiny narrow-billed Todies, with their Caribbean mix of emerald green and scarlet red feathers. Under the huge hourglass that shaded the Boulevard, children from Saint-Marc shared the last news, played soccer and billiards, hide-and-seek or lago, and rode their bikes among the ylang-ylang and timimi flowers.

"Your father was happy to run errands for Madame Willy—the old woman who would not accept charity. Goule bought things he didn't need from her shop—dusty bedsheets, a few glasses, an embroidered tablecloth. And one day, this is what happened…"

Listening to her stories, it was less that I found it impossible to escape from Papa's shadow than that I found it impossible to even try. I wrote about Papa with demonic patience—ruthlessly reapplying myself to the material. My stories were about wanting and how there is no end to it.

"Are you writing about your father?" Mother asked. Her forehead ribbed with worry. "Leave it alone."

She'd found me at the typewriter and didn't want me awake tonight. She brought a fresh blanket, which she tucked around me in bed, and kissed my forehead. She touched my hair lightly, like she thought I was sick. She scratched her temple with one fingernail like a record skipping over some song she'd have loved to remember, one she seemed to never give up on. I pulled the cover over my head when she said, "Lights out," and I prayed for sleep. The curtains caught their breath, hinges hummed. I wondered what a Cereus flower smelled like.

At Saut Mathurine, in Camp-Perrin, Papa tried to teach me how to swim in the green cavern. At eighteen, I loved the water's irresistible chiaroscuro, the weight of its insistent pressure, that willingness to embrace a stranger. Each breath I took, amplified by water, crashed against my eardrums. The water opened, swallowed me, until I mirrored the sky and had no memory, no future, just the loose flesh of water.

Around the waterfalls and along the trail leading to them, we spotted various varieties of flowers, birds, and plants.

"Look," Papa said. "A Cereus plant."

Now he saw them everywhere.

When we returned home, my father sat next to me on the balcony and peered at the Reina de la noche from beneath the low visor of his hand.

"When the night bloomer blooms," he said, "you forget how ugly and unruly this plant can be, and your patience seems worthwhile."

Papa watched me in delight, the smile on his face, child-like. It was probably the same smile he had years and years ago, the day his brother took him horseback riding in Saint Marc. Papa recalled the smell of the wild ferns and the wind that blew against his face.

That one day on a horse's back—short but memorable like a Cereus flower in bloom.

My mother's Reina de la noche was in a porous, unglazed clay pot—those were best, as they allowed the soil to dry rapidly and also provided extra bottom-weight to the top-heavy plant. Mother fertilized once a year in late spring. The stems had a disorganized, unpredictable growth habit. Some trailed across the floor, broad and wavy. Others, pencil-thin, with rootlets sprouting along their sides, shot straight up from the soil and reached the ceiling of the balcony in a matter of weeks.

Laying by the Cereus plant, I read the daily papers (the death toll rose); I listened to my parents chat with the neighbors and friends and relatives about the violence, the tortures, the disappearances, the beatings, the shootings, the protests, the strikes. They said the country would explode, but la vie continue. A reporter on TV was interviewing a police officer about the killing of a young girl in Delmas. The commissaire rubbed the side of his face, the way high-ranking police officials tend to do when they sympathize but can't (or won't) help. The vacant and narrow-faced father spoke in a monotone voice as if reporting from the moon. The dead were by that point either singing with choirs of angels or sitting in the eternal workshop of hell.

Years ago, on her deathbed, Man Simone had asked me to send her letters. "I want to know you," my grandmother had said in a whisper, the last time I visited her in Saint Marc.

I had promised to write, meant to do it, but never got around to it.

I looked at the princess and wondered about the somebody I might be, or should be, or could be. I was a shadow. My face was, to put it mildly, forgettable; I was the girl with her hand half-frozen in a wave at an acquaintance who failed to recognize her.

Papa had a full beard of white foam, and I liked the slow, scraping sound of the razor's straight blade, the menthol smell of the shaving cream, and the swish of the water as he rinsed his skin. He finally told me about Saint Marc; he described the hopscotch squares traced with chalk on the sidewalks, the pitter-patter of feet landing on rhymes, how he'd water his mother's rosemary till he could smell it on his fingers. I imagined him in Man Simone's vegetable garden— his shirt a stained dust rag, his fingernails filling with dirt, his hands brushing the tickle from his forehead. As a kid, he'd learned to fry plantains and griyo.

"There's no part of a pig that can't be used," he said as I imagined the plantains hitting the pan, thrilling.

The clouds outside his home in Saint Marc were churning and the earth was furred with grass beneath the trees. I could smell the water in the ditches, see the moon a white hole in the aqueduct, stars freckling the irrigation puddles.

I watched Papa out of the corner of my eyes. The hands holding the razor were thick and coarse, with drying lines and rough calluses, with dark veins and enlarged knuckles. The fourth finger of his left hand was swelling around the wide gold wedding band. I didn't think he could get the ring off. My father's hands were expressive and large as they gestured his memories.

I imagined my parents as young lovers, she in a sundress, he in shorts, nonchalant in their summer skins. Mother showed me a photograph. This was a picture that stilled Papa's sadness long enough in the play of light and shadow at afternoon's end, in the edge of evening. I wanted to hold him. His neck was smooth as the girdled part of a Cereus plant. I imagined the muffled noise of branches budding.

The buds trumpeted upward. Early in the afternoon, flesh-colored sepals loosened, showing a hint of snowy petals at the open end. At sunset, the blossoms opened, and by midnight they achieved full display, dangling heavily against bright, glossy, green stems.

Mother, Sœur, and I stood in awe, in our nightshirts, watching each flower move as it opened. We'd opened a bottle of Manischewitz to celebrate.

Papa came out and hugged me. I didn't push him away.

twenty-five

The scholarship letter from Barry University in Miami, Florida, arrived on a Friday.

I danced with the fat envelope in my hands, and my body swayed, boneless, all liquid and waves. My insides must have sounded like water skimming backwards across the sand into the thick of the ocean I'd be soon flying above.

"I didn't know you'd applied for a transfer," Mother said. Her voice cracked.

Sœur drew a deep, shuddering breath. "You're leaving."

"It's a good thing," Papa said.

I nodded. And they nodded, reassured of their know-how, their ability to take a problematic situation and fix it. Mother held the letter—the promise of freedom.

I dropped out of med school.

I would become a writer—a High Priestess of the Written Word.

That night, I turned from side to side until I'd kicked off the covers. I remade the bed and tucked myself in again. Switched on the light, turned it off, fluffed my pillows, threw them off. I drank milk, read Marcel Pagnol and Jacques Stephen Alexis, tried a telenovela on Univision. I told myself again and again: I'm leaving Haiti. I'm leaving—alone. I whispered it into my mirror. Screamed it into my sheets. I'm leaving Haiti. At five in the morning, exhausted, I lay flat on my back, relieved to succumb to sleep.

I packed *all* of my belongings. Even that dress a bit passé, layers and layers of organza, a stiff dress, the kind you'd leave behind to travel light. I was waking up from the long sleep of childhood.

Mother cried, bent double on the toilet seat. She listened to Michel Sardou and Charles Aznavour, and her sadness blended into the song.

"She's sad because you're almost gone," Papa said, shutting the door. "Don't bother your mother."

His nightly theatrics had ravaged his vocal chords. He'd been yelling at my mother again, but I no longer saw him as this volatile storm, this one-dimensional man who used his own sad childhood stories to justify his violence against the woman he swore to love "until death do us part." Yes, he had spent years using tales of his own father's sour temper like currency, his difficult upbringing as both trump card and disclaimer, but I'd come to understand Papa and the weight he carried inside.

Papa drove me to the airport and we passed row after row of concrete houses. I was about to step into the unknown, out of a past that might be stripped away from me like clothing. I looked at my father—rangy, temperamental, twitchy with impatience. I played with the radio knob, tried to find a station, but got static and a soccer game. I shrugged and leaned back. Long stretches of road went by; I was off in some reverie—my mother's kiss when I'd said goodbye, the way her eyes held mine, the smile too bright.

We went through several roadblocks erected on the long, busy roads between Thomassin and Port-au-Prince, where police checked for licenses, drugs and firearms. Haiti still fell apart. Even before the next tragedy struck, we could feel its presence hanging in the air as heavy as the mosquito spray we used at night.

As we reached the airport, the air was thick with fog, as dark clouds lowered themselves like a shroud. Somehow the breeze—such a small, insignificant thing—was enough to conjure a memory. I imagined myself behind the wheel of the Jeep, cutting into the open space in front of large trucks on the Road of Thomassin, driving 100 mph in the mountains, a daredevil trying to escape my father's realm of violence. I thought of all the guys I dated in my life: Junior, whose unstable mother threatened to rip me apart; Ben, who was fifteen years older, and into lurid phone sex; Pierre—thoughts rising out of my belly; and ultimately Dave in his constant haze. Some of these relationships had been a way to get back at Papa, who wanted me to meet un homme de bonne famille, a gentleman from a nice family.

Memory is mutable. Faces slipped into and away from me, impossible as holding onto water. The world, in that moment, was closing in, trying to detain me, clamp me down like a bug. I spread my fingers evenly over my skull and pushed inward and counted to one hundred. I wanted to forget about my parents' fights: the shoves and loud words, my father's hands—broad, sweaty and cold—hands that tried but somehow never succeeded in smashing my mother's jaw and breaking her ribs. I wanted to forget about the violence that cocooned the rise into power (and subsequent fall) of Jean-Bertrand Aristide, the gunshots at night that forced me to roll out of my bed and on to the floor.

Outside the airport, intense heat and a mob scene greeted us. About twenty men surrounded us, elbowing each other to grab my bags and carry them. I could see my luggage go off in different directions as I kissed Papa on the forehead, put my arms around him, locked my fingers, and told him, "I'll miss you." Part of me wanted these words to be true.

Papa had the neutral face he wore between waves of emotion. Rage, perplexity, nostalgia: three gears he more and more frequently idled between. I would not have guessed I'd prefer anger to absence. As he walked back to the car, leaving me with two men to carry my bags, I saw that the set of his shoulders was not from anger, but sadness; it was sadness that made him walk this way. And I felt something close to love.

But soon, that thing, that moment, was over, leaving no evidence of itself behind. A woman stood beside me, surrounded by flies—a buzzing cloud that flirted with the stray scents that came down the alleys.

"Bonswa, Jessica," she said. Good afternoon.

I didn't recognize her at first. Felicie, our old housekeeper, had become skeletal, her body thinned to sharp-boned essence, her eyes sunk deep into shadows.

She put down her basket on the sidewalk. "Listen, listen," she said. "My godsons are dead. All three. Pitit sè mwen mouri."

She needed to speak the words aloud.

The breath drew up in my throat and my skin went clammy. My hands useless and folded in front of me, I listened intently to Felicie, nodding, cocking my eyebrow, biting my lip, opening my eyes wide.

For years after she'd left our home, Felicie had awoken at the first breath of dawn to sell bananas, kachiman and mangoes at the market so her godsons could become teachers, doctors, lawyers. They'd become thugs, instead, and they'd been killed.

The wind blew and her blouse fluttered as if a bird, trapped inside, were trying to get out. Her eyes blurred with tears. "All of them—dead," she repeated, "dead." She told about how she'd worried about them. With the palm of her hand, she'd check their breathing, her hand rewarded with the rise and fall of their backs. She'd watch them sleep—listened to them sleep, a sound like a valve opening and closing.

"Mademoiselle, are we going?" one of the men holding my bags asked. He held out his hand for a tip.

"In a minute."

Cars in the street passed in a steady stream, and ı wondered how many people in them had lived through someone dying as a result of violence here. Felicie carried on. When her children were sick, she'd stay awake thirty-six hours, her guts twisting with worry. When they came home from school, she'd hug them tightly, enfold them too long. She'd prayed for them at night, the white plastic breads of her rosary sweating lesions into her hands.

A car flew by, sending up a cloud of dust that drifted toward us. Felicie coughed, waved her hand, and turned away from the road. She looked dazed, exhausted. She talked about Antoine, her godson, the quick kiss they'd exchanged the morning of his death, not enough, not a full good bye—and that was the last time she saw him alive. Felicie couldn't change that end, go back, walk with Antoine a little longer.

Her mouth opened, but no words came out. Her hands flailed like helpless, dying things at the ends of her arms. She shivered. And I shivered too. Felicie stared into space, and I looked upward with her. We looked up at the sky. We stayed quiet for a moment, breathing, until the man asked again, "Mademoiselle, are we going?"

Felicie raised the basket to her head. "All of them," she murmured. "Dead."

She didn't wait for me to hug her. She walked slowly down the street, not wanting to get home where no one would surround her. The house was quiet, I was sure, and sometimes during the darkest of night she probably woke up because it was just that, too quiet.

Guilt weighed on me for leaving Port-au-Prince.

Down the road, she stopped short, turned to look at me, and then continued walking, stopped, and looked back again. I caught her eyes. I wanted to remember her face and honor Felicie somehow for what she showed me: raw pain, the ground zero of being human. I was connected to her. Loss reminds us that we're alive—makes us feel our own lives more acutely for a while.

twenty-six

January 2010.

Some things have not changed—the crunchy gravel of the dirt roads, the rooster's crow, the buzz of bees, the bright yellow sun of the Haitian dawn. The rest is spooky in its familiarity, yet wrong in detail. A chill settles onto the top of my stomach. Even my skin has gone cold. I drive holding the steering wheel close, among the crowds of unwashed faces and the men asleep against their stomachs, the makeshift tent villages. Sometimes, a humanitarian truck barrels up behind me and rides my tailpipe.

In Turgeau, where rubble still blocks many streets, I slow down to look for the crumpling of recognizable memory. That's the time when I should blame God, wonder if He got angry for being mocked, if His patience simply ran out—the moment when I should decide He sees us all, unblinking. But I can't stop believing in His love and I am angry for this faith I carry around like excess baggage.

As I park the car on Jean Paul II Avenue, I remember la Fête Dieu. In my childhood, many streets in Turgeau would be closed to traffic so devoted Christians could assemble the magnificent carpets of flower petals, pine needles, and palm fronds. At six o'clock in the morning, a procession of Roman soldiers mouthing sorrowful songs, and of purple-robed penitents carrying a statue of Jesus on the cross, paraded in front of the houses, destroying the carpets, a great honor for those who worked at night creating them. One year, as a teenager, I took part in the procession and fell in love with one of the boy soldiers. That day, I beseeched God to allow me to marry a good man, a non-violent man, different from my father, so I could walk down the aisle of Sacré Coeur in a billowy white dress.

Now my city is lost, the ground covered in dusty, dry blood.

The burning sun toasts my body. I stand across the street from what used to be Dynamic Club, the place where I exercised in my adolescence. At the time, all I knew about health was how to bandage a small wound. I could barely stabilize a broken limb or find a vein, let alone administer a drip. Even before med school, I drove to Dynamic Club to lift weights and run on the treadmill. I drove my first car around Turgeau, a red Isuzu Trooper that did not always stop when you pushed the brakes.

It was in front of Dynamic Club one day that I noticed the small bullet hole in the rear window of the Isuzu. A silver filigree of cracks ran from the edges and into the safety glass. I thought of Jesus dressed in a fine white suit, sitting in the passenger's seat, bleeding. I believed He kept me safe from the sneaky shooter.

It was after a session at the Club one afternoon that I got sick over the death of Junior, a loss that had occurred years before I'd gotten over my adolescent infatuation with him. I got so upset I puked on the side of the road. Then there was nothing left inside me; I gagged—my bowels clutched and spasmed but all that came out of me was thin yellow liquid. Light-headed, I was losing the feeling of my body.

Years have passed, carrying their own blessings and curses. I'm known to dwell on the past, not to let things be, to worry about who what why when, so my father often reminds me that everything in life is pre-ordained, that a correct order exists in the events of this world. I want to believe him. I've been driving around Port-au-Prince, looking for some sign that this—the earthquake, the desolation that follows it—is not random. I need a face to hold on to. I want to look an unknown person in the eye, past my own incoherent grief, my own futility.

A man stands next to me. He's in his forties, wearing shorts and an engaging smile. "I'd just come back from Dynamic Club when it happened," he says. "I'd changed into clean clothes and was playing the drums." He turns to point at the house behind us. A pile of rubble. "This is my home," he says. "I had to dig my way out." He sighs. "The house is destroyed, but it's still my home."

Pedestrians wave at the man. "Moscoso, sak pase?"

A wide, easy grin spreads across his face. "We've lived in Turgeau forever. Everyone knows me around the neighborhood. It's good that they know I'm still around. Otherwise looters would dig up what's been buried." Across the street is the collapsed funeral home Pax Villa, where I attended Junior's viewing.

He is a jolly and playful man, Moscoso, with a laugh as quick as his smile. He erases the bad stuff. There is something about his posture, something dignified, quiet, and settled.

I walk to the end of the street, along the lip where the asphalt falls away into a narrow ditch. I reach Sacré Coeur, where my mother and I recited our Credo on Sunday mornings. Father Israel said mass there. From my apartment in Miami, I tried Father Israel's cell phone after the earthquake. I wanted to speak about religion and God, discuss the meaning of life. I remember he loved beautiful things. He kept shelves of leather-bound novels, poetry, and art books in his study. Father Israel had long, strong fingers like those that should play a harp.

He didn't pick up. As the phone burned in my hand, I tried to remember the instant before I learned about the earthquake, the ordinary moment when I leaned against my pillows, watching *Family Guy* in my home in South Florida. Until the phone calls and the TV newscasts about dead bodies and rubble, the moment was indistinguishable from the hundreds of other occasions when I'd turned on the TV and laughed at Stewie, the cartoon.

A large cross remains standing outside the church. Which is a kind of beauty. I fear the Jesus on the cross, as I did as a child. He looks peaceful, yet threatening. I study the smooth shape of his hands, his face with its beatific expression. I hope to stop believing then, and start cursing God. But the fear goes away.

The roof is still intact, but walls have fallen in. I walk inside the ruins and take in the smell of rotten flesh. The pews are covered with dust. A cell phone and a New Testament have been left behind. Afternoon sunlight streams through a crack, and dust particles whirl and jig across the beam, thousand floating up with each new footprint on the dusty floors.

The church is destroyed, but this is still the house of God. Eyes closed, palms pressed together beneath my chin, I mouth a Hail Mary.

When we lived on Christ-Roi Street, not far from Turgeau, my mother and I often visited Sacré Coeur, and every Sunday I hoped to emerge translucent and Catholic, clean as philosophy. The stillness of Christ crucified, candles smoking, Lenten draperies. Rosary clanking. One of the priests often paced the aisles during the sermon, his eyes searching for sinners. When he stopped, my heart stopped. I tried to be still, unnoticed as a candle before it burns. For many years after that, I positioned myself at a safe distance from God and Satan, tempting both, until I grew closer and closer to God because of that room in the human heart that's older than the body. Sometimes, though, I wish I'd gone the other way so I could freely cry, "Treason!"

I ache for the peace faith doesn't bring.

"There's still a body stuck in that hallway," a voice says. The voice is that of a young man in cut-offs. His hands are thick-veined. He watches me as he smokes a cigarette. He's got a growth on his neck, shiny and red—a smooth round lump.

He points at a caved-in passage. "The body is right there." His mouth splits into an exaggerated smile, rows of teeth. Then he hides it behind his hand and giggles, head bobbing like the bobbin of thread on Mother's sewing machine. He inhaled a slow drag, the cigarette firm in his lips, and I watched the sudden surge of orange at the tip.

"Any word about Father Israel?" I ask.

He shrugs. "Father Israel is fine. *Just fine.*"

Maybe it's true. Or maybe he doesn't know who Father Israel is.

Some people begin to sing outside, huddled in the church garden beneath the sun's hot glare. In another reality, the hymns surrounding me would lift me up. But heat overwhelms me as I stand, stunned, in the fierce, dry air. I go back to the street, walk around. Out here, the huge blue sky looms above us, bigger than ever, like it might swallow the rest of us up.

The naked crazy guy who walks by me does not see me. No one pays attention to me—not the three-legged dog or the old beggar. I watch the slow breath of the dog on its side; he stretches, legs raised so all three touch the wall, each paw making little shivers. The place where its leg once was is healed over and covered with fur, weirdly beautiful. I wonder if the dog hates the missing leg for leaving.

I hear the flick of a lighter behind me and smell the stream of smoke as the man in cut-offs exhales. I can see into the channel of his ear, a narrow darkness spiraling deep inside his head. He tells me dogs can feel earthquakes coming. Before the ground shook, the dogs in Port-au-Prince barked and whined, nervous, restless. As he tells me this, the man's eyes jump in the sockets, not completely focused.

"Not everything is lost," the man with the lump says.

He's not looking at me. But maybe he's talking to me. Maybe I will heal, even without understanding or belligerence.

acknowledgements

I want to thank Dan Wakefield, professor and friend nonpareil, and source of great support, great counsel, and encouragement. My gratitude to John Dufresne for his guidance. I am indebted to the very patient Les Standiford who cheered me on to the finish line. Special thanks to Bruce Harvey and Debra Dean, whose suggestions and advice have been invaluable. Thank you, Edwidge Danticat, Johnny Temple, and Lynne Barrett, for your support.

I also owe a debt of gratitude to Vicki Hendricks, Kim Barnes, M. Evelina Galang, and Madeleine Blais, who had faith in me and who encouraged me as a writer at a time when I needed it most. I will never forget your kindness.

Merci, mèsi, gracias to friends and family who read and commented on this memoir as it was written. A million thanks wouldn't be enough. Your feedback on the various drafts of my memoir pushed me to be more honest to myself and to my readers. Special thanks to Corey Ginsberg, Fabienne S. Josaphat, Laura "Stella" Richardson, Rebecca N. Carmant, Joe Clifford, and Ellen Ullman for their careful comments and critiques of the entire manuscript.

Thank you, Les Stone and Charlotte Howard, for your artistic talent. Thank you, Kathie Klarreich, Michael Tarr, and Claude Rousseau, for your help with my research. Thank you, Marie-Ketsia Theodore-Pharel and Mahalia Solages, mes inlassables cheerleaders.

Thank you, Raptor Jesus.

I want to extend my appreciation to the entire MFA community at Florida International University, to the Miami Poetry Collective, to VONA/Voices at the University of Miami, to Lip Service, and to the gang of *Sliver of Stone Magazine*. It's an inspiration to work with such a talented and giving group of writers.

Thank you, Matt Peters and Melanie Neale: I fell in love with Beating Windward as soon as I met the both of you.

I send my love to God, to my mother Carmita, to my wonderful sisters Nathalie, Jennifer, and Patricia, to my aunt Marlène, to my cousins Marie-Christine and Clarissa, and to Hector Lominy Jr. And finally, in memory of Man Simone and Man Clara, my grandmothers, and my father, Julio.

Thank you to the editors of the following anthologies in which excerpts from this memoir appeared: *Haiti Noir* (Akashic Books, 2011) edited by Edwidge Danticat, *Reflections on Home* (Holy Cow Press, 2013) edited by Jim Perlman, Deborah Cooper, Mara Hart, and Pamela Mittlefehldt, and *The Beautiful Anthology* (TNB Books, 2012) edited by Elizabeth Collins.

Sections of this book also appeared in the following literary journals: *The Mom Egg* (Volume 8: Lesson), *Tupelo Quarterly* (Issue 7: Pilgrimage, Voyage, and Return), *The Caribbean Writer* (Volume 25), *The Southeast Review* (Volume 29.1), and *The Nervous Breakdown*.

about the author

Born in Port-au-Prince, M.J. Fievre self-published her first mystery novel, *Le Feu de la Vengeance*, at the age of sixteen. She was nineteen years old when she signed her first book contract with Hachette-Deschamps, in Haiti, for the publication of a Young Adult book titled *La Statuette Maléfique*. As of today, M.J. has authored nine books in French. Two years ago, One Moore Book released Jessica's first children's book, *I Am Riding*, written in three languages: English, French, and Haitian Creole.

In addition to book-length texts, M.J. also writes short stories, essays, plays, and poems. She's included in *Une Journée Haïtienne*, edited by Thomas C. Spear. Her short stories and poems in English have appeared in various anthologies and magazines, including *15 Views of Miami* (Burrow Press, 2014), *The Beautiful Anthology* (TNB Books, 2012), *Haiti Noir* (Akashic Books, 2011), *The Mom Egg*, *The Southeast Review*, *Saw Palm*, *The Caribbean Writer*, and *Daily Bites of Flesh: 365 Days of Flash Fiction*. She's a regular contributor to the online journal *The Nervous Breakdown*. Two of her stories in Spanish are forthcoming in a Bolivian mystery anthology. She was featured last year on Buzzfeed and was a writer-in-residence at the Betsy Hotel. Her story, "Sinkhole," which appeared in *15 Views of Miami*, was nominated by the Pushcart Board of Contributing Editors for the Pushcart Prize. Her play, *To Accept, Dial 5 Now*, was performed at MicroTheater Miami during the O, Miami Festival.

M.J. is also an editor. In 2010, she founded *Sliver of Stone Magazine*, a well-loved, bi-annual, online literary magazine dedicated to the publication of work from both emerging and established poets, writers, and visual artists from all parts of the globe. In 2012, she edited *So Spoke the Earth*, a multilingual anthology about Haiti, which explores the country's past, present and future as experienced by 54 contributors, for an eclectic, international combination of established and emerging writers. This important anthology about Haiti is a celebration of Haitian spirit, multiculturalism and diversity.

In 2013, with Nicholas Garnett and Corey Ginsberg, M.J. edited *All That Glitters*, a *Sliver of Stone Magazine* nonfiction anthology. As a board member of the publishing house, Lominy Books, she organizes a yearly writing contest in French, encouraging aspiring writers in Haiti to pursue their dream. In fact, she often returns to Haiti to conduct writing workshops for middle and high school students. She's regularly featured at both Livres en Folie (LEF) and Foire Internationale du Livre d'Haiti (FILHA), two annual book fairs in Haiti. In 2014, she served as judge for a contest organized by the Bureau du Secrétaire d'Etat à l'Intégration des Personnes Handicapées (BSEIPH) and also presented her books at Femmes en Création, in Bourdon.

M.J. moved to the United States in 2002. She obtained a Bachelor's Degree in Education from Barry University and an MFA from the Creative Writing program at Florida International University. She taught writing for 8 years at Nova Middle School in Davie, and later became a writing professor at Broward College and Miami Dade College. She's been a key note speaker at Tufts University, in Massachusetts, at the Mom Egg Reading, in New York, at the Haitian Book Fair in Washington, D.C., at AWP, in Washington, and at Michael College, in Vermont. Last year, she spent a semester in Santa Cruz de la Sierra, in Bolivia, where she taught writing at the International University. While in South America, she was invited to conduct a seminar at the Alliance Française on the Myths and Legends of the French Antilles, and all her novels in French are available at the Alliance Française de Santa Cruz.

M.J. has always been active within the South Florida community. A few years ago, with artist Jean-Michel Daudier, she organized several editions of Haiti Out Loud, a night of poetry and music in Pembroke Pines. She's taught ekphrastic poetry and haiku workshops at the Miami Art Museum, and in various schools, including iTech @ Thomas A. Edison Educational Center, in Miami, and Tedder Elementary, in Pompano Beach. She's an ambassador for Lip Service, a John S. and James L. Knight Foundation award-winning organization and a Miami institution. She's also a proud member of the Miami Poetry Collective, famous for its Poem Depot, a regular feature of Wynwood's Second Saturday Art Walk.

She's participated to the Miami Book Fair International on several occasions. She's also presented her books at Haiti en Livres, the Anancy Festival, and the South Florida Book Festival, and at various literary events at Miami City Hall, Miami Dade College, Broward College ("Caribbean Week" and "Literary Feast"), and the University of Miami. She was a speaker at different events organized by the Consulate General of Haiti for "Mois de la Francophonie." She's served twice as a judge for the "Dis Moi Dix Mots" Contest launched by the Cultural Departments of the Consulate General of France and the Consulate General of Haiti, in Miami, for students in the "French Heritage Language Program" and those attending partner universities in Miami. As an alumna of the Miami chapter of VONA (Voices of Our Nations), a workshop for writers-of-color, M.J. contributed to the anthology *Dismantle*, published by Thread Made Blanket. Her blog, The Whimsical Project, gets about 150 hits every day.

M.J. continues to serve the community by working as a certified Haitian Creole court interpreter for the 11th Judicial Circuit. She has not retired as a teacher, however: She's a facilitator for Exchange for Change, teaching creative writing at a women correctional facility. She's an educator who wrote several educational scripts for the University of Miami, Department of Epidemiology and Public Health. The scripts, turned into short films, were written in both English and Haitian Creole and aim at educating the Little Haiti community about diabetes, cervical cancer, and the HPV vaccine. M.J. was interviewed by the University of Miami for the Haitian Diaspora Oral History Collection, which includes videos and selected transcripts of oral history interviews conducted with individuals of Haitian ancestry that are well-renowned in the world of the arts. She's also included in Florida's International University's Digital Library of the Caribbean.

In March 2015, M.J. received the "Beacon of Hope and Achievement Award" from the Consulate General of Haiti in Miami.

CPSIA information can be obtained
at www.ICGtesting.com
Printed in the USA
LVOW12s1556010416

481756LV00004B/467/P